INSTRUCTOR'S MANUAL TO ACCOMPANY

Breaking Through: College Reading

Ninth Edition

Brenda D. Smith
Georgia State University, Emerita

LeeAnn Morris
San Jacinto College

with contributions by
Carolyn Poole
San Jacinto College

Longman
New York   Boston   San Francisco
London   Toronto   Sydney   Tokyo   Singapore   Madrid
Mexico City   Munich   Paris   Cape Town   Hong Kong   Montreal

Instructor's Manual to accompany Breaking Through, Ninth Edition, by Brenda Smith and LeeAnn Morris
Copyright © 2010 Pearson Education, Inc.

All rights reserved. Printed in the United States of America. Instructors may reproduce portions of this book for classroom use only. All other reproductions are strictly prohibited without prior permission of the publisher, except in the case of brief quotations embodied in critical articles and reviews.

1 2 3 4 5 6 7 8 9 10—OPM—12 11 10 09

Longman is an
imprint of

www.pearsonhighered.com

ISBN 10: 0-205-63965-8

ISBN 13: 978-0-205-63965-6

CONTENTS

PREFACE

This book is designed to help students develop learning strategies to achieve success in college reading, and to transfer those successful learning strategies to other college courses.

Organization of the Chapters in
Breaking Through: College Reading

Breaking Through opens with a chapter that describes the motivation, the actions, and the "mind set" needed for success in college. Chapter Two concentrates on theories of reading and the strategies used by good readers. Reading is thinking and interacting with the printed page in three stages: before, during, and after the process.

Chapter Three is dedicated entirely to vocabulary development, introducing and providing exercises on vocabulary building strategies such as using context clues, word parts, the dictionary, the glossary, the thesaurus, and analogies.

The most important reading comprehension skill is understanding the main idea. Chapter Four contains many practice exercises that move from the general to the specific in explaining this skill. Chapter Five reinforces the main idea skills with models, explanations, and practice exercises on the recognition of significant details, patterns of organization, and the beginning stages of notetaking. Chapter Six focuses on reading to learn and explains annotating, notetaking, outlining, and mapping.

Awareness and practice can improve test scores and give a winning edge. Chapter Seven helps students become aware of how tests are constructed and what is expected in the test-taking situation. It provides opportunities for application and practice.

Chapter Eight, on efficient reading, includes exercises to assess student reading rates and presents techniques for rate improvement. The characteristics of good students are again discussed in Chapter Nine, with an emphasis on the college student as an analytical reasoner and problem solver. Exercises are provided to help students develop and refine their analytical reasoning skills. Chapters Ten and Eleven explain implied meaning and focus on unstated attitudes and assumptions. These two chapters are designed to help students become more critical of what they read and more aware of suggested meaning and how writers can manipulate their audiences.

Each chapter is designed to be a self-contained teaching unit so that instructors can skip around and teach the skills in the order that best fits their needs. One chapter is not necessarily dependent on another, although some follow more logically than others.

A case book follows Chapter 5 and asks the burning philosophical question for students to ponder, "What is beauty?" Students begin with an inventory to document present beliefs and end with a similar inventory to assess change. The organization of the case book differs from the regular chapters by having several short reading selections followed by reflective, open-ended questions. The goal is for students to problem solve, reflect, and grow.

Organization Within Each Chapter

Most chapters follow a similar format. A reading skill is introduced and discussed, and short exercises are presented for practicing the skill. Then the new skill is applied to longer selections from college textbooks. Thirteen selections, including three new ones, along with new and expanded exercises provide students with additional practices. Answers to the exercises appear in the Annotated Teacher's Edition. Grade Level Equivalencies (GLEs) for the longer reading selections have been added to the Annotated Teacher's Edition as another tool to assist instructors in selecting reading selections appropriate for their students' abilities. GLEs were determined using the Raygor Readability Estimate.

The selections are followed by comprehension and vocabulary questions, as well as other open-ended questions for written responses. The comprehension questions ask for literal and inferential meaning and are designed to promote an understanding of the passage. The vocabulary words are listed in the phrases in which they appear. A line number is listed to note where the word appears in the selection so the student can refer to the larger context. Vocabulary enrichment activities are at the end of the longer selections to reinforce the skills presented in Chapter Three. The feature, Interpret the Quote, provides students with opportunities to hone their critical thinking skills by applying thought-provoking quotes to the longer reading selections and then, after reading the selection, thinking and writing about how the quote relates to the selection. Each chapter also suggests ways to incorporate My Reading Lab and Reading Workshop to both strengthen reading skills and develop reading for pleasure.

Nine of the chapters end with vocabulary lessons centered around developing a family of words through a knowledge of word parts.

This ninth edition of *Breaking Through* includes the entire textbook chapter, "Leadership and Management" from John R. Walker's, *Introduction to Hospitality*, Fifth Edition. Found in Appendix 1, it gives students an opportunity to apply the lessons learned throughout *Breaking Through* on a chapter from a freshman-level textbook. This additional practice chapter prepares the students for the types of reading they will encounter in freshman-level courses. The pages of the book are perforated so that students can tear out assignments and give them to the instructor for further evaluation. Responses to the reflection, essay, and summary items particularly need the individual attention of the instructor.

Preview Items

Always introduce and overview assigned readings. Use the introductory paragraph preview questions to stimulate interest and to activate schemata. Remember that prior knowledge is the strongest predictor of reading comprehension. Corroborate for students that they do indeed know something about or related to the subject and help them realize that they must bring their own experience and knowledge to the printed page.

Written Response Items

The "React," "Reflect," "Think Critically," and "Think and Write" questions following the selections offer opportunities for written responses. The "React" questions are positioned directly after the reading to encourage students to immediately recall and interact personally with what they have read. The "Reflect" items probe for the significance of the information, and the "Think Critically" questions explore the application of the material to other situations. "Think and Write" questions reach for broader generalizations in connecting the new knowledge with the ideas in the introductory paragraph.

Vocabulary Development

In addition to Chapter Three on vocabulary building, the vocabulary items at the end of each selection, and the vocabulary enrichment exercises, the nine vocabulary lessons (one in each chapter of the *Instructor's Manual*) contain true-false, matching, and fill-in-the-blank vocabulary items that can be used to stimulate thought before reading or to provide feedback after reading and studying the words.

Everyday Reading Skills

At the end of each chapter is a section that focuses on reading needs students encounter in daily life. The topics include print media, electronic media, contemporary fiction and nonfiction, mnemonics, workplace reading, personal mail, and reference works. The purpose of these sections is to apply general reading skills to everyday life situations and provide students the strategies to become enlightened consumers and critical thinkers. A list of Everyday Reading Skills is included in the Instructor's Manual.

Collaborative Problem Solving

Four questions appear at the end of each *Breaking Through* chapter to provide collaborative applications and critical thinking opportunities that reflect the content of the chapter. Challenge students toward intellectual contributions. These activities can be motivating, stimulating, enlightening, and entertaining. Prior to assigning the activities, discuss group dynamics. Explain the characteristics of responsible leadership and group membership. Several enlargements on these topics are included in this *Instructor's Manual* for transparencies to assist you in classroom discussions.

Insist that each group use a transparency for recording ideas to promote focus and clarity. After allowing group discussion time, ask one speaker or the total group to stand before the class and report the responses. Watch the time carefully to be sure that each group has the opportunity to report.

You can provide the transparencies and markers, or you can require that students purchase them at the bookstore when buying textbooks. The transparency method forces group decision making because of the need to get something written down to create the visual aid. During the presentation, the transparency provides a level of organization that does not always occur when students speak. The method also gives students practice in a lifelong business skill for successfully presenting material to groups.

Reader's Tip Boxes

These boxes condense strategies for improving reading and studying into practical hints for quick reference. An enlarged version of each box is included in the *Instructor's Manual* for you to copy onto a transparency for classroom presentations. Tips for reading and studying in specific college disciplines are inserted directly before the first longer selection in that particular discipline.

My Reading Lab

Each chapter includes a reminder to students to go to MyReadingLab.com and complete the corresponding Reading Road Trip activities. The *Instructor's Manual* also has suggestions for using the other online resources such as the Pearson Vocabulary and Study Skills Web sites.

Reading Workshop

In the Reading Workshop, students are encouraged to read novels and reflect on their reading through a Reading Workshop Journal. With the goal of developing lifelong readers while building schemata, hopefully students will see the value in reading for pleasure. A handout that fully explains Reading Workshop is included in the Instructor's Manual. Each chapter contains suggestions for incorporating Reading Workshop into the classroom. Additional suggestions are found in each chapter of the *Instructor's Manual*.

Vocabulary List

In order to provide a quick reference, the vocabulary words that are included in the questions at the end of each longer reading selection are listed in alphabetical order at the end of this manual. The chapter and selection in which the word is used is indicated for quick reference.

Variety of Content Area Materials

The selections were chosen to represent a typical variety of college courses. The content areas are represented as follows:

Psychology	Art
Business	Computer Science
Journalism	Criminal Justice
English (Essays and Short Stories)	Speech

Sociology	Political Science
History	Health
Communications	Nutrition
Science	Journalism

Additional Quizzes in the *Instructor's Manual*

The *Instructor's Manual* contains a short true-false quiz on comprehension and vocabulary for each longer reading selection. In some cases, the comprehension questions are not very difficult and students may be able to answer them without reading the passage. On the other hand, some of the questions demand a thorough reading. Depending on the selection, you might use the questions in any of the following ways:

1. As a preview to be used before reading the selection.
2. As a method of beginning class discussion.
3. As a check to see whether students read and understood the selection.

Regardless of your purpose in using the questions, on some occasions you may want to call them out orally to help students sharpen their listening skills. Tell students that you will say a question once, repeat it once, and will not go back. The first two or three times you do this, a few students will ask you to repeat. Tell them you are sorry but you can't. After that they will listen more attentively and understand the questions the first time around. If you use the questions orally, for the sake of time, you may want to pick only five of the comprehension and five of the vocabulary questions.

If time is an issue, the questions can be distributed. In this edition, the questions are arranged on a separate page so that you can copy them for a class quiz or for individual students. When using the copier, fold back the answers. Be sure to collect the questions from students so that the quizzes do not "float."

Overheads for Class Discussion

Several pages are included that can be copied on transparencies and used on an overhead projector to direct class discussion. A list of overhead transparency masters for these as well as the Reader's Tips boxes appears on pages xi-xiii.

Personal Feedback Connection

Retention research has shown that success in college is not just about academics; it is also about the personal well-being of each student. Many freshmen orientation programs, for example, stress the importance of students finding a "significant other" adult on campus who can serve as a mentor and friend. Thus, the purpose in including the Personal Feedback questions is more personal than academic, although the questions are a mix of both. If students will respond in a serious manner, the answers can offer the instructor a wealth of information on the personal and academic struggles of each student. Even if you are not particularly comfortable with some of the questions, try them and see if the answers help you help your students. To encourage responses, consider giving students 5 to 10 points for answering each assigned page, and assign enough sections to total 100 points. You can then use this grade as a quiz or test grade.

Instructor's Manual on Instructor's Resource Center

Instructors can download this *Instructor's Manual* from the catalog Web site (http://www.pearsonhighered.com/devenglish) with a login name and password. If you do not have a login name and password, visit the Instructor Resource Center at www.pearsonhighered.com to register.

TRANSPARENCY MASTERS AND READER'S TIPS FOR CLASS DISCUSSION

EVERYDAY READING SKILLS BY CHAPTER

Learning Tools in the *Instructor's Manual*

Introductory Classroom Materials. Samples for a number of introductory classroom materials are included in this Instructor's Manual, based on material that has been used in the classroom. These materials are included to serve as models and may or may not reflect the needs of your curriculum. Please feel free to copy these materials and adjust them to your own institutional and curriculum needs. The materials include the following:

Class Outline. A sample semester outline is included to provide a possible model for developing your own timeline. Change the specifics to fit institutional differences and your own course requirements.

Sample 4th Week and Mid-Semester Evaluation Forms. Feedback throughout the semester can be rewarding and informative. The timing works in your favor and gives you the information to ensure that students end the course with a positive experience. This feedback allows you to find out about individual concerns, address them, and make appropriate changes that can strengthen the course.

Sample Feedback Form for Presentations. If you assign classroom presentations, you can distribute these forms so that each student, as well as you, can give constructive feedback in organized categories. Each of these categories should be discussed before the presentation.

Effective Leadership and Group Membership Characteristics. Using a transparency, discuss this material with students prior to group activities or immediately after the first group session.

Class Visitation Assignment. To build student awareness and self-confidence, assign a visit to a 100- or 200-level lecture course. Ask students to not only take organized notes on the lecture but also to take notes on student behaviors. Grades will be based on a combination of the reports on the two activities. A complete explanation of the assignment is included for you to distribute to students. I view this assignment as a capstone experience. I make it in the second half of the semester after completing instruction on main idea skills. Give students plenty of advance notice so that they can select an appropriate class—which is an assignment in itself. Students who pick interesting classes love this activity, and those who don't learn about the value of investigation before registration. For your own course planning, consider that this is an excellent assignment to leave with students when you attend a professional conference. You can be assured of an active discussion upon your return to class.

Student Information Sheet: Have students complete a profile sheet the first day of class. This provides you with potentially valuable information as well as current contact information. For instance, it has been the experience of many instructors to find that phone numbers on file with the institution are not current.

Participation Journal: Borrowed from Skip Downing's *OnCourse Workshop* materials, the participation journal has proven to be a valuable classroom tool for monitoring student learning and class involvement. Each day before leaving class, students complete two sentences: "Today, I learned…" and "I earned my participation points today by…." One suggestion for the journal use is to staple it in a folder for each student. Students pick up the folder as they enter the classroom and drop it off as they leave. It takes only a couple of minutes to go through the folders and 'grade' them at the end of each class. Students quickly learn to be specific in their responses if they want full credit. The journal grade can be part of the attendance/participation grade.

Reading Journal Assignment Sheet: This document fully explains the Reading Workshop Journal and includes a sample journal entry and vocabulary chart.

IDEAS FOR THE CLASSROOM: SAMPLE MATERIALS

Samples for classroom materials that have been used in the classroom are included in this *Instructor's Manual*. Please feel free to copy these materials and adjust them to your own institutional and curriculum needs. These materials include the following:

- Class Outline
- Student Feedback Form for Presentation (Can be used by the instructor and students)
- Sample 4th Week Evaluation
- Sample Mid-Semester Evaluation
- Effective Leadership and Group Membership Characteristics (transparency master)
- Class Visitation Assignment
- Student Information Sheet
- Participation Journal
- Reading Workshop Assignment Sheet

CLASS OUTLINE
15 week semester
1 1/2 hour class—twice a week

For sample purposes only; actual page numbers may be different.

Week 1   CLASS 1:
Introduction to course
Go over syllabus
Introduction of students
Students journal—write about their reading strengths and weaknesses
Homework:
Read Chapter 1 (pages 1–29)
Fill in weekly activity chart (page 10)
CLASS 2:
Chapter 1, "Student Success"
Homework:
Feedback 1, 2, 3 (pages 3, 6, 14)
Reading 1 (pages 3–5), exercise 1 (page 5)

Week 2   CLASS 1:
Chapter 3, "Vocabulary"
Introduce vocabulary for quiz (page 71)
Homework:
1. Exercises 9–10 (pages 91–93)
CLASS 2:
Chapter 3, "Vocabulary"
Homework:
1. Study for 1st vocabulary quiz (page 71)
2. Reading Road Trip—Visit The Library of Congress, Washington, D.C.
    Do practice exercises and mastery tests

Week 3   CLASS 1:
1. Vocabulary Quiz 1 (page 71)
2. Introduce Vocabulary Quiz 2 (page 108)
Chapter 2, "Stages of Reading"
Homework:
1. Read "Food Allergy or Food Intolerance" (pages 51–55).
    Do comprehension (1–10) and vocabulary (1–10).
2. Demonstrate with written notes (in your book) the way you use the 5 thinking
    strategies (page 35) as you read "Food Allergy or Food Intolerance."
CLASS 2:
Chapter 2, "Stages of Reading"
Comprehension Quiz, "Food Allergy or Food Intolerance"

Homework
1. Study for Vocabulary Quiz 2 (page 108)
2. Read "Galvaston Disaster," (page 57–61).
Do comprehension (1–10) and vocabulary (1–10)
3. Reading Road Trip: visit Bourbon Street, New Orleans.
   Do practice exercises and mastery tests.

Week 4   CLASS 1:
Vocabulary Quiz 2 (page 108)
Introduce words for Vocabulary Quiz 3 (page 168)
Comprehension Quiz, "Galveston Disaster"
Chapter 4, "Main Idea," (page 115)
Homework:
1. Read "Sleeping and Dreaming," (page 141–148)
   Do comprehension (1–10), vocabulary (1–10), and vocabulary enrichment (1–10)
2. Read first assignment for Textbook Chapter
CLASS 2:
Comprehension Quiz, "Sleeping and Dreaming"
Chapter 4, "Main Idea" (page 115)
Discuss first reading assignment from Textbook Chapter
Homework:
1. Read "Shatterproof," (page 149–158).
   Do skill development (1–10), vocabulary (1–10)
2. Reading Road Trip: Visit The Maine Woods and do practice exercises
3. Study for Vocabulary Quiz 3 (page 168)

Week 5   CLASS 1:
Chapter 4, "Main Idea," (page 115)
Vocabulary Quiz 3 (page 168)
Introduce words for Vocabulary Quiz 4 (page 238)
Comprehension Quiz, "Shatterproof"
Homework:
1. Review Chapter 4 for your Main Idea test.
2. Reading Road Trip: Visit The Maine Woods and do mastery tests
CLASS 2:
Main Idea Test (TB: pages 21–28)
Homework:
1. Read "The Dream of Nonviolent Reform," (page 152).
   Do skill development (1–4), comprehension (1–10), vocabulary (1–10)
2. Study for Vocabulary Quiz 4 (page 531)
3. Do Search the Net, (page 166). Pick one of the two assignments.

Week 6   CLASS 1:

Vocabulary Quiz 4 (page 238)

Introduce words for Vocabulary Quiz 5 (page 311)

Quiz on "The Dream of Nonviolent Reform"

Chapter 5, "Supporting Details and Organizational Patterns"

Homework:

1. Read "Becoming Healthy," (page 212–219) and do comprehension (1–10), vocabulary (1–10)
2. Read second assignment for Textbook Chapter

CLASS 2:

Comprehension Quiz, "Becoming Healthy"

Chapter 5, "Supporting Details and Organizational Patterns"

Discuss second reading assignment for Textbook Chapter

Homework:

1. Read "Let Them Eat Cake," (pages 229–236) and do comprehension (1–10), vocabulary (1–10), vocabulary enrichment (1–15)
2. Study for vocabulary quiz 5 (page 311)
3. Reading Road Trip: Visit Ellis Island and The Statue of Liberty. Do practice exercises and mastery tests.

Week 7   CLASS 1:

Chapter 8, "Efficient Reading" (page 349)

Vocabulary Quiz 5 (page 311)

Comprehension Quiz, "Let Them Eat Cake"

Homework:

1. Study for midterm
2. Reading Road Trip: Visit The Indianapolis Speedway. Do practice exercises and mastery tests.

CLASS 2:

Midterm on Textbook Chapter

Homework:

Study for Vocabulary Quiz 6 (page 343)

Week 8   CLASS 1:

Vocabulary Quiz 6 (page 343)

Introduce Chapter 6, "Textbook Learning," (page 290)

Homework:

1. Read "Behavior Change," (page 283). Do comprehension (1–10), vocabulary (1–10), and vocabulary enrichment (1-15).
2. Reading Road Trip: Visit Seattle. Do practice exercises and mastery tests.

CLASS 2:

Comprehension Quiz, "Behavior Change"

Chapter 6, "Textbook Learning," (page 290)

Homework:
1. Study for Vocabulary Quiz 7 (page 421)
2. Read "Goya Foods," (page 292). Do comprehension (1–10), vocabulary (1–10), and vocabulary enrichment (1–15).
3. Reading Road Trip: Visit Spring Break. Do practice exercises and mastery tests.

Week 9   CLASS 1:
Vocabulary Quiz 7 (page 421)
Introduce words for Vocabulary Quiz 8 (page 489)
Comprehension Quiz, "Goya Foods"
Chapter 7, "Reading Casebook," (page 423)
Homework:
1. Reading Road Trip: Visit The Grand Canyon. Do practice exercises and mastery tests.
CLASS 2:
Chapter 7, "Test Taking," (page 317)
Homework:
1. Reading Road Trip: Visit The Grand Canyon. Do practice exercises and mastery tests.
CLASS 2:
Chapter 7, "Test Taking," (page 317)
Homework:
1. Study for Vocabulary Quiz 8 (page 480)
2. Reading Road Trip: Visit Hollywood and do practice exercises and mastery tests.

Week 10   CLASS 1:
Vocabulary Quiz 8 (page 480)
Introduce vocabulary for Quiz 9 (page 533)
Chapter 10, "Inference" (page 441)
Homework:
1. Read "The Best Place" (page 457). Do comprehension (1–10), vocabulary (1–10), and vocabulary enrichment (1–15)
CLASS 2:
Comprehension Quiz "The Best Place"
Chapter 10, "Inference" (page 441)
Homework:
1. Study for Vocabulary Test 9 (page 553)
2. Read "The Alchemist's Secret" (page 466). Do thinking after reading (1–8) and vocabulary enrichment (1–10).

Week 11

CLASS 1:
Comprehension Quiz "The Alchemist's Secret"
Vocabulary Test 9 (page 533)
Chapter 10, "Inference" (page 441)
Homework:
1. Study for Inference Test
CLASS 2: Inference Test (TB: pages 49–58)
Homework:
1. Reading Road Trip: Visit the Grand Canyon. Do practice exercises and mastery tests.

Week 12

CLASS 1:
Chapter 11, "Critical Reading"
Homework:
1. Read "The Dinner Party" (pages 511–517). Do comprehension (1–10), vocabulary (1–10), and vocabulary enrichment (1–15).
CLASS 2:
Comprehension Quiz, "The Dinner Party"
Chapter 11, "Critical Reading"
Homework:
1. Read "Cosmetic Surgery for Pets" (pages 519–524). Do comprehension (1–10), vocabulary (1–10), and vocabulary enrichment (1–10).

Week 13

CLASS 1:
Comprehension Quiz "Cosmetic Surgery for Pets"
Chapter 11, "Critical Reading" (page 485)
Homework:
1. Read "We'll Go Forward from this Moment" (pages 527–533). Do comprehension (1–10), vocabulary (1–10), and vocabulary enrichment (1–10).
CLASS 2:
Comprehension Quiz, "We'll Go Forward from this Moment"
Chapter 11, "Critical Reading" (page 485)
Homework:
1. Reading Road Trip: Visit The Getty Museum. Do practice exercises and mastery tests.

Week 14

CLASS 1:
Reading Casebook
Homework:
1. Read "Pushing Past Trauma to Forgiveness" (pages 435–439). Do comprehension (1–10), Complete Forgiveness Inventory (page 439).

CLASS 2:
Review for Final Exam—ATP Level 1 Form A (pages 1–10). This is to be completed in class as practice for final exam.
Homework:
1. Study for Final Exam
2. Use My Skills Lab for extra practice for final exam.

Week 15   CLASS 1:
Last Class: Make up vocabulary test for students
Students verage their grades
CLASS 2:
Final Exam ATP Level 1 Form B (pages 11–20)

- Also included in the My Skills Lab is the Longman vocabulary Web site and Longman study skills site. These can be independent home or class exercises for the student.

- Class exercises will be a mixture of group work, independent work, and exercises and exercises done and explained as a class.

- You will be expected to volunteer in class or to read and answer questions.

Student Feedback Form

Name of Presenter _____

Circle the number that best evaluates the presentation in each area.
(5 is highest or best and 0 is lowest.)

Organization of information	5	4	3	2	1	0
Presenter's knowledge of topic (research)	5	4	3	2	1	0
Physical and vocal aspects	5	4	3	2	1	0
Quality of transparency/handouts	5	4	3	2	1	0

Overall Rating: Excellent __ Very Good __ Good __ Needs Improvement __ Poor __

Comments _____

_____

Student Feedback Form

Name of Presenter _____

Circle the number that best evaluates the presentation in each area.
(5 is highest or best and 0 is lowest.)

Organization of information	5	4	3	2	1	0
Presenter's knowledge of topic (research)	5	4	3	2	1	0
Physical and vocal aspects	5	4	3	2	1	0
Quality of transparency/handouts	5	4	3	2	1	0

Overall Rating: Excellent __ Very Good __ Good __ Needs Improvement __ Poor __

Comments _____

_____

Student Feedback Form

Name of Presenter _____

Circle the number that best evaluates the presentation in each area.
(5 is highest or best and 0 is lowest.)

Organization of information	5	4	3	2	1	0
Presenter's knowledge of topic (research)	5	4	3	2	1	0
Physical and vocal aspects	5	4	3	2	1	0
Quality of transparency/handouts	5	4	3	2	1	0

Overall Rating: Excellent __ Very Good __ Good __ Needs Improvement __ Poor __

Comments _____

4ᵗʰ Week Class Evaluation for: Course _____

Please take a few moments to provide feedback on how you are finding the course and any suggestions for improvement that you may have. Written comments are especially helpful to us.

Please do NOT write your name on this form.

Student Preparation for Class   Please circle:

1. Do you understand what is expected of you to prepare   Yes   Sometimes   No
    for and participate in class session?

2. Do you review the class notes at home?   Yes   Sometimes   No

3. Do you ask questions when you do not understand material?   Yes   Sometimes   No

4. When you have the lecture notes ahead of time, do you read
    them before lectures?   Yes   Sometimes   No

5. Do you work on homework assignments with other students?   Yes   Sometimes   No

6. Are you usually well prepared for class?   Yes   Sometimes   No

7. Do the assignments make sense to you?   Yes   Sometimes   No

8. Outside of lectures and textbook sections, how many
    hours per week do you spend on reading, computing,
    homework, etc. for the class? _____ hours

9. What would help you to learn the material better?

Your View of Course

10. In your opinion, what is working well about this course?

11. What would you change about the course?

Mid-Semester Evaluation

Directions: Do not sign your name. Please answer each question honestly. This is your opportunity to have input into the format of the class and in the direction and process of my teaching. This will not impact your grade in any way. Respond using the following scale:

strongly agree	agree	neither agree nor disagree	disagree	strongly disagree
1	**2**	**3**	**4**	**5**

1. My professor speaks clearly.   1 2 3 4 5

2. The explanations of the material are clearly stated.   1 2 3 4 5

3. The professor cares that I understand the material.   1 2 3 4 5

4. The professor encourages questions.   1 2 3 4 5

5. The professor clearly communicates the expectations of the course.   1 2 3 4 5

6. I am comfortable asking my professor a question in class.   1 2 3 4 5

7. I am comfortable seeking help from my professor outside of class.   1 2 3 4 5

8. I do my assignments almost every night.   1 2 3 4 5

9. I attend class regularly.   1 2 3 4 5

10. I have done my best in this class.   1 2 3 4 5

11. My present grade in this course is: A B C D F

Comments:

Source: Nessmith, C. M., & Watkins, P. C. "Transitions in Teacher Evaluation: A Model for Peer Review." NADE/GA Conference, Augusta, GA, April 21, 1997.

Effective Group Leadership and
Group Membership Characteristics

Be an Effective Leader

- Value people.

- Listen actively.

- Be tactful and respectful.

- Give credit and praise.

- Be consistent in treatment of others.

- Admit mistakes.

- Keep a sense of humor.

- Set a good example.

Be an Effective Group Member

- Pool your talents with the group.

- Listen respectfully and with an open mind.

- Critically evaluate individual ideas.

- Make sure you understand and are understood.

- Be willing to change your thinking.

- Remember that conflict is a natural part of group communication.

- Disagree with an idea, not with a person.

Adapted from *Human Communication*, by Joseph DeVito, p. 329

Class Visitation Assignment

Directions: Attend at least an hour and a half of a 100- or 200-level lecture course. You may choose the course and time you attend. Please introduce yourself to the professor and ask permission. The purpose of this exercise is twofold. First, you will have an opportunity to take notes in an actual class setting along with other students who are trying to be successful. Secondly, you will be able to observe student behaviors and draw your own conclusions about the relationship of the behaviors to academic success.

Grade: This assignment has two parts. Each part is worth 50 points and should include the following information:

Part 1: Class Notes

Take notes on the class lecture as if you would be studying the material for an exam. Your notes should be organized to indicate main ideas and significant details. Your grade will be based on content, organization, and the understanding you are able to convey about the material. Try to attend a class in which the professor gives a lot of notes. Do not attend a mathematics class or a class that is having an exam.

Part 2: Reflect on Student Behaviors

Carefully observe the behavior of students in the class you are visiting. Take notes on what you notice. For example, are students paying attention? Do students arrive late? If so, does it matter? Are students taking a lot of notes? Do they ask questions? Do they talk to one another? What surprises you? What did you expect? What behaviors do you feel will foster success, and what behaviors will hinder success? Describe several students specifically. After the class use your notes on students' behaviors to write a summary about your observations. This should be organized into paragraphs and be no more than two pages and no less than one page.

Have fun!

Name _____   Class _____

Student Information Sheet

1. Name as registered for the course: _____

2. Name preferred to be addressed by: _____

3. Phone numbers: Day _____   Evening _____

4. Family Information: _____

   _____

5. Interests? (sports, hobbies, pastimes) _____

6. Employed? Where? _____ In what capacity? _____

   How many hours a day? _____ How many days a week? _____

7. Which word describes your computer skills?

   Non-existent _____ Rookie _____ Semi-expert _____ Expert _____

8. Do you have a computer at home? _____ Internet at home? _____

9. What is your ultimate degree and employment objective? _____

10. What do you see as your strengths? _____

11. What do you see as your weaknesses? _____

12. Name something you have done of which you are proud. _____

13. Any special problems (reading disabilities, medical problems, family and/or job concerns, etc.) of which I should be aware? _____

    _____

14. What would you most like to learn in this course? _____

    _____

15. Class schedule: (Include course number, course name, days/times, and instructor). Use the back of the sheet if necessary.

Name _____

Participation Journal

Date	Today I learned…	Pts.	I earned my participation points by…	Pts.

READING COMPREHENSION
RESPONSE JOURNAL INSTRUCTION SHEET

Reading: One of the best ways to improve your reading skills is to form the reading habit. All college educated adults should strive to be 'readers.' You will need to read for a minimum of a half hour each night. We will also be reading in class.

Books: You choose your own books. I prefer that you make your selection from the classroom collection of paperbacks, but if you wish to buy your own books, please check with me first. You are to have a book in your possession at all times. If you don't like a book, abandon it and choose another.

Part 1: Journal entries: Three times a week you should write in your response journal. Do NOT tell what the story is about. Use the suggestions below to help you decide what to write. One week's entries should be approximately one page in length. For example, if there are two weeks between times to turn in your journal, you will need to turn in about two written pages (six entries). Grades will be assigned according to the number of entries and total pages written as well as the quality of your responses. The best journals reflect serious thinking about the reading rather than superficial summaries of what happens in the book. If you are stuck, try these suggestions. Remember to vary your responses. You might want to write about:

1. Any passage that puzzles you
2. Items that intrigue you
3. How the material makes you feel
4. What you think might happen next
5. What you think the author was like
6. Why you think a character acted like he/she did
7. What you think it would be like to live in this setting
8. Your reaction to a character or event
9. Something the reading reminds you of
10. The way the story is written
11. What you might have done differently if you were the author or the character
12. What makes the writing effective/ineffective
13. Something you learned from the reading (facts and/or insights about life)

Part 2: List of words in context: Each time you turn in your response journal you will include a list of five words that you want to make part of your vocabulary. These should be words you have come across in your reading. Record the work/source with page number and the sentence in which it is used. Write what you think the word means from the context. Next, check the dictionary meaning to see if your definition is accurate; write it down, too. Don't interrupt your reading to do this; make it a separate activity.

SAMPLE JOURNAL ENTRIES (partial)

Date: July 12

Title / Author: Turtle Moon, Alice Hoffman

Time read: 12:30 – 1:30 pm, pages 1 – 32

I like the way Hoffman uses words; it's almost like poetry. Her descriptions make it easy to imagine the setting. For example, when she talks about the humidity in Verity, Florida, she says the air is so thick that "sometimes a soul cannot rise and instead attaches itself to a stranger…" Just like Houston!

Date: July 13

Title / Author: Turtle Moon, Alice Hoffman

Time read: 12:15 – 1:00 pm, pages 51 – 70

I'm not sure yet what Janey Bass has to do with the murder or what her relationship to Julian is. It's obvious there is a lot of tension between her and Julian. I have a feeling he might be the 'bad boy' she was in love with in high school. Julian is sure a strange character. His ability to communicate with his dog and to track suspects is almost supernatural. Something must have happened to make him so obsessed.

Date: July 15

Title / Author: Turtle Moon, Alice Hoffman

Time read: 1:00 -2:00 pm, pages 102 -135

I suspected from the beginning that Julian might be just the right person to get through to Keith. Keith's mother is trying so hard to do the right things for him, but a mother isn't always capable of providing what 13 year old boy needs, just because she is his mother. Keith may be the 'meanest boy in Verity,' but he is really just confused. I think Julian can reach him through the dog.

SAMPLE WORD LIST (partial)

Elation

Turtle Moon, p. 9: "Keith feels a wicked surge of <u>elation</u>."

Meaning in context: excitement?

Dictionary meaning: great joy

Antinomy

Article in *American Psychologist*, p. 118; "The <u>antinomy</u> between basic and applied research was being rejected."

Meaning in context: conflict?

Dictionary meaning: contradiction between two reasonable laws

ANCILLARY MATERIALS

Book-Specific Ancillary Materials

FOR INSTRUCTORS

Annotated Instructor's Edition (AIE) (0-205-63964-X)
An exact replica of the student text, with answers provided on the write-in lines in the text.

Instructor's Manual (0-205-63965-8)
Offers teaching tops, sample syllabi, and other teaching resources.

Printed Test Bank for *Breaking Through*, Ninth Edition (0-205-63966-6)
Offers a series of skill and reading quizzes for each chapter; formatted for ease of copying and distribution.

Developmental Reading Student Supplements

PRINT SUPPLEMENTS

Q: Do you require a dictionary and/or thesaurus?

The Oxford American Desk Dictionary and Thesaurus, 2/e (0-425-18068-9)
From the Oxford University Press and Berkley Publishing Group comes this one-of-a-kind reference book that combines both of the essential language tools—dictionary and thesaurus—in a single, integrated A-to-Z volume. The 1,024 page book offers more than 150,000 entries, definitions, and synonyms so you can find the right word every time, as well as appendices of valuable quick-reference information including: signs and symbols, weights and measures, presidents of the U.S., U.S. states and capitals, and more.

The Oxford Essential Thesaurus, 1/e (0-536-35520-7)
From Oxford University Press, renowned for quality educational and reference works, comes this concise, easy-to-use thesaurus - the essential tool for finding just the right word for every occasion. The 528 page book includes 175,000 synonyms in a simple A-to-Z format, more than 10,000 entries, extensive word choices, example sentences and phrases, and guidance on usage, punctuation, and more in exclusive "Writers Toolkit."

Q: Could your students use a quick-reference review sheet containing the vocabulary skills?
Vocabulary Skills Study Cards (0-321-31802-1)
Colorful, affordable, and packed with useful information, Longman's Vocabulary Study Card is a concise, 8 page reference guide to developing key vocabulary skills, such as learning to recognize context clues, reading a dictionary entry, and recognizing key root words, suffixes, and prefixes. Laminated for durability, students can keep this Study Card for years to come and pull it out whenever they need a quick review.

Q: Could your students use a quick-reference review sheet containing the basic reading skills?
Reading Skills Study Card (0-321-33833-2)
Colorful, affordable, and packed with useful information, Longman's Reading Skills Study Card is a

concise, 8 page reference guide to help students develop basic reading skills, such as concept skills, structural skills, language skills, and reasoning skills. Laminated for durability, students can keep this Study Card for years to come and pull it out whenever they need a quick review.

Q: Do you require your students to have a planner?
Pearson Student Planner (0-205-66301-X)
This useful supplement provides students with a space to plan and think about their work with a working area (including calendars, studying tips, and other valuable materials), and a daily planner for students including daily, weekly, and monthly calendars.

Q: Do you require your students to have a journal?
The Longman Reader's Journal, by Kathleen McWhorter (Student / 0-321-08843-3)
The first journal for readers, The Longman Reader's Journal offers a place for students to record their reactions to and questions about any reading.

Q: Would a student-friendly guide on study skills be beneficial to your course?
10 Practices of Highly Effective Students (Student / 0-205-30769-8)
This study skills supplement includes topics such as time management, test taking, reading critically, stress, and motivation.

Q: Do you like to use additional textbook readings in your course for students to apply their reading skills?

TEXTBOOK CHAPTERS

The Longman Textbook Reader, Second Edition (with answers Student} (0-321-48629-3) or (without answers Student) (0-205-51924-5)
Offers five complete chapters from our textbooks: computer science, biology, psychology, communications, and business. Each chapter includes additional comprehension quizzes, critical thinking questions, and group activities.

The Prentice Hall Textbook Reader (0-13-184895-X)
This supplementary reader includes eight complete college textbook chapters from a variety of disciplines. Each chapter includes a one-page introduction to the selection and various exercises after the selection.

Q: Would you like to use literature in your class to develop your students reading and writing skills?

Longman Literature for College Readers Series

This collection was designed to maximize students' reading and writing abilities through a rich literature collection by a diverse array of authors. Each text guides developmental readers step-by-step through mastering works of fiction and nonfiction by surrounding the selections with rich pedagogy, including exercises, questions, and writing prompts.

Longman Literature for College Readers Series
This collection was designed to maximize students' reading and writing abilities through a rich literature collection by a diverse array of authors. Each text guides developmental readers step-by-step through mastering works of fiction and nonfiction by surrounding the selections with rich pedagogy, including exercises, questions, and writing prompts.

Literature Anthologies (edited by Yvonne Sisko)
American 24-Karat Gold 3/e (0-205-61765-4)
Looking at Literature (0-321-27670-1)
Sterling Stories, 2/e (0-321-36523-2)
World of Stories, 2/e (0-205-61766-2)

Longman Annotated Editions

Appelbaum / Sisko (editors) *Dracula (Longman Annotated Novel)* (0-205-53308-6)
Coleman / Sisko (editors) *The Scarlet Letter (Longman Annotated Novel)* (0-205-53252-7)
Davis / Sisko (editors) *The Red Badge of Courage (Longman Annotated Novel)* (0-205-53253-5)
Doss / Sisko (editors) Frankenstein *(Longman Annotated Novel)* (0-205-53309-4)
Sisko (editor), *The Secret Adversary (Longman Annotated Novel)* (0-205-53256-X)

Penguin Discount Novel Series

In cooperation with Penguin Putnam, Inc., Pearson is proud to offer a variety of Penguin paperbacks at a significant discount when packaged with any Pearson title. Excellent additions to any developmental reading course, Penguin titles give students the opportunity to explore contemporary and classical fiction and drama. The available titles include works by authors as diverse as Toni Morrison, Julia Alvarez, Mary Shelley, and Shakespeare. To review the complete list of titles available, visit the Pearson-Penguin Putnam website: **http://www.pearsonhighered.com/penguin**.

Q: Do you like to use advice resources written by students for students?

Students Helping Students® Series

These helpful guides, written and edited by college students and recent grads, allow current students to learn from their peers' experience. The candid, practical advice gives a straightforward story on how to deal with challenges and get through college. (Show list at www.etipsforagrades.com.)
Titles include:
Navigating Your Freshman Year
Have No Career Fear
Fishing for a Major
Getting Through College without Going Broke
Choose the Right College and Get Accepted
Tackling the College Paper

Q: Do you like incorporating multimedia in order to enhance your student's learning experience?

Multimedia Offerings

Interested in incorporating online materials into your course? Longman is happy to help. Our regional technology specialists provide training on all of our multimedia offerings.

Pearson MyReadingLab (http://www.myreadinglab.com)
MyReadingLab (www.myreadinglab.com)
Powered by two reading practice engines, the new version of MyReadingLab provides diagnostics, practice, tests, and reporting on reading skills from the best selling Reading Road Trip and on student reading levels with the Lexile Framework for Reading developed by Metametrics™, an educational measurement expert.

Reading Skills, based on the best-selling reading skill tutorial Reading Road Trip, has been thoroughly revised and redesigned with added and revised exercises, a new mastery-based format, open-ended questions, and the instructor's ability to reorganize the arrangement of topics.

A newly added Lexile system (modified Cloze-tests and scoring algorithms) developed by MetaMetrics permits instructors to assess students' reading levels, and offers quantifiable data to measure reading level advancement.

Personalized student study plans within MyReadingLab are made for students based on results of the diagnostic pre-test and organization of topics established by the instructor.

Comprehensive assessment is available for students and instructors. Students can monitor their progress via their personal gradebook; instructors monitor progress at the individual level or class level.

In addition to the unparalleled practice MyReadingLab offers, students also receive complimentary access to three acclaimed Pearson websites: Vocabulary Website, Study Skills Website, and Research Navigator.

Specifically created for developmental reading students, *MyReadingLab* is the first online application that combines diagnostics, personalized practice and tests, and powerful assessment tools to help improve student *reading skills* and *reading level*.

FLEXIBILITY

MyReadingLab is a powerful, easy-to-use program that allows instructors to target their specific course goals, while enabling them to spend more time teaching and less time preparing and grading exercises. From arranging topics to determining the amount of available sets or readings to establishing mastery scores, *MyReadingLab* empowers instructors to control the delivery of the practice to their students.

DIAGNOSTICS

Available in both the reading skill and the reading level areas, the diagnostics in *MyReadingLab* build personalized study plans for each student. The Reading Skill diagnostic pre-test assesses students' strengths at the individual skill level. The Reading Level diagnostic provides students with an initial "Lexile" measurement, which instructors and students can use to measure reading level progress through the semester.

PERSONALIZED STUDY PLAN

Each student's study plan is generated by the results of their diagnostic pre-tests and the topic organization established by the instructor. The study plan appears in an easy-to-reference "To Do" list format that helps students stay on track while working in *MyReadingLab*.

GRADEBOOKS

All work in *MyReadingLab* is captured in the site's easy-to-use Gradebooks. Students monitor their work, and instructors can track the progress of an individual student or an entire class via detailed reports. Multiple gradebook reports show results depending on the exact needs of the instructor or student.

THE INSTRUCTOR GRADEBOOK contains several types of reports:

- **THE CLASS SUMMARY** shows performance details for each student in the course and enables instructors to view several items, including time on task, mastery status for each student, and averages for all exercises and diagnostics.

- **THE TOPIC SUMMARY** shows how many students have mastered each topic. Instructors can also view class averages for all exercises and diagnostics sorted by topic. Using this snapshot of results, instructors can pinpoint weak spots and plan lectures accordingly.

- **THE ALERTS** area lets instructors know when a student has exhausted all the exercises for a topic without achieving mastery, alerting instructors to students who may be having difficulty.

THE STUDENT GRADEBOOK provides students with an archive of their exercises and test sets, so they can access them for review.

- **THE STUDENT DETAIL REPORT** shows student scores on all of the exercises in this course, which include the readings, the questions, and the student responses.

- **THE DIAGNOSTIC DETAIL REPORT** shows students scores on each of the diagnostic tests in this course.

myreadinglab

To MyABL Labs Kowalski   Teacher View   Settings   Help   Logout

Course: *DEMO Populated Gradebook - , Intermediate: 9-12th grade level*
Instructor: Ta MyABL Labs Kowalski

| Home | Study Plan | Gradebook |

Home > Study Plan > Purpose and Tone - The Getty Museum, California

Purpose and Tone - The Getty Museum, California

Before you arrive at California's magnificent Getty Museum, you'll be doing a bit of preparatory reading. In order to fully understand what you are reading, you will need to be able to recognize the author's purpose. An author's purpose for writing might be to inform, entertain, persuade, etc. For example, a news article about the Getty Center may have been written to inform the public about this important cultural resource. When you are able to identify an author's purpose you will have also gained clues for determining the work's tone, recognizing slanted language, and identifying an author's point of view or bias; all of which help you to gain a greater understanding of what you have read.

POINT OF INTEREST

Review Materials				
① Overview: Purpose and Tone	View			
② Model: Purpose and Tone	View			
Activities		**Score**	**Sets Available**	**Sets Taken**
③ Practice *	New Set	83%	4	2
④ Test *	New Set	100%	4	1

✱ = Required

Return to Study Plan

myreadinglab

To MyABL Labs Kowalski   Student View   My Courses   Settings   Help   Logout

Course: *DEMO Populated Gradebook - ,Intermediate: 9-12th grade...

| Home | Study Plan | Submissions | Gradebook |

Home Page > Gradebook Options > Class Summary > Student Detail

Reading Skills Details for SWYK Student1
The student detail report shows this student's performance on all topics and exercises in this course.

Summary			
Mastered in Diagnostic:	0	Pre-test Avg:	22%
Mastered in Course:	1	Post-test Avg:	0%
Not Mastered:	14	Required Exercise Avg:	85%

| Reading Skills | Reading Level | Score: Recent |

X Clear Diagnostics   Icon Key   Export   Print

Topic	Mastered	Time on Task	Practice	Test	Pre	Post
Main Idea - Maine Woods		00:06:14	80		0	
Inference - Great Lakes Region			75		25	
Purpose and Tone - The Getty Museum, California					0	
Vocabulary - The Library of Congress, Washington, D.C.					0	
Active Reading Strategies - New Orleans, Louisiana	✓	00:08:23	100	90	•	•
Supporting Details - The St. Louis Arch, Missouri					40	
Outlining and Summarizing - Spring Break in Florida					25	•
Patterns of Organization - New York Harbor					40	
Critical Thinking - American Southwest					50	
Reading Textbooks - Grand Canyon, Arizona		00:14:06	80		•	•
Graphics and Visuals - Wall Street, New York					•	•
Reading Rate - Indianapolis Speedway, Indiana					•	•
Memorization and Concentration - Mount Rushmore, South Dakota					•	•
Note Taking and Highlighting - Seattle, Washington					•	•
Test Taking - Hollywood, California					•	•

PRACTICE

The extensive and effective practice opportunities in *MyReadingLab* come in two basic types:

• practice with the discrete skills to improve students' **READING SKILLS.**
• practice combining multiple skills in a single reading passage to improve students' **READING LEVEL.**

READING SKILLS

Students practice reading skills through a mastery-based format in which they get an overview of the skill, see models of the skill at work, go through an abundance of practice exercises to apply what they've learned, then take a mastery test. Among many skill topics are main idea, supporting details, inference, outlining and summarizing, and active reading. Exercises include objective questions, open-ended questions, short answer questions, and combined skills exercises.

READING LEVEL

MyReadingLab assesses reading level using the Lexile Framework (www.lexile.com). This framework measures both reader ability and text difficulty on the same scale. First, a student completes a carefully developed diagnostic, and then the system assesses it to assign an initial Lexile level or number. Next, the student works through *MyReadingLab* and completes two types of exercises: combined skills and "cloze." Combined skills exercises test 15 different skill areas (for example, active reading or supporting details). Cloze questions ask students to identify words that have been deleted from passages of text, thereby testing how well a student can apply context, comprehension and knowledge of vocabulary. The overarching goal is for a student to increase his or her Lexile reading level and overall reading skills while working through *MyReadingLab*.

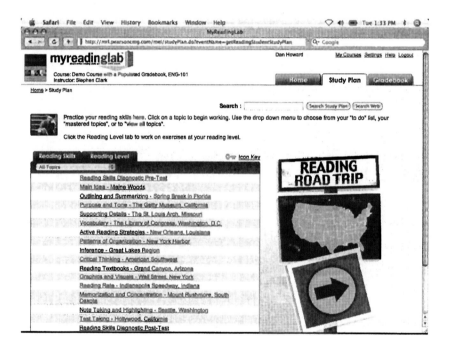

TRAINING
Training is an integral part of the Pearson Media program.
Local on-campus training
Schedule an on-campus faculty training with your local Pearson representative. Training sessions are tailored to prepare you and your colleagues to successfully implement *MyReadingLab* in your reading courses. Ask about our First Day of Class student orientation.

Weekly Online Training
Every Friday there is an interactive, online training for *MyReadingLab*. Please check the website for the exact time. Simply call in, log on, and a member of the *MyReadingLab* content team will:

- guide you through the lab
- demonstrate all the features
- answer any questions you may have about integrating *MyReadingLab* into your course

To participate in an online training session, please visit www.myreadinglab.com and follow the instructions in the "Learn About" section.

For more information, including a video walkthrough of features, please visit www.myreadinglab.com and click on the "Learn About" tab. Or contact your Pearson representative to schedule a demonstration.

Do you want to become a stronger reader?
Do you want to track your progress in your reading course?
Do you want to get a better grade?

MyReadingLab has helped students all over the country improve as readers and succeed in college. MyReadingLab will help you become a better reader and help you get a better grade too!

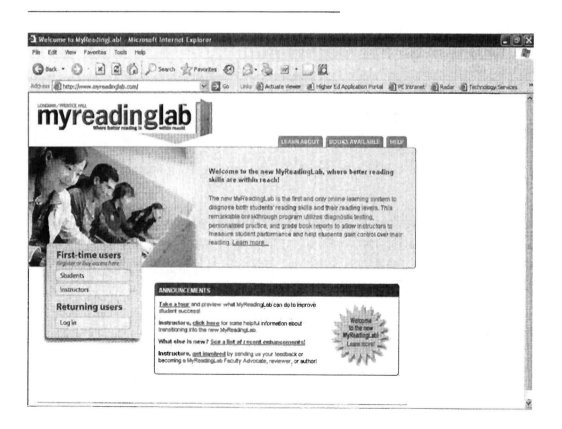

www.myreadinglab.com

REGISTER ...

It is easy to get started! Simply follow these easy steps to get into your MyReadingLab course.

1) **Find Your Access Code** (it is either packaged with your textbook, or you purchased it separately in the bookstore or at www.myreadinglab.com). You will need this access code and your COURSEID to log into your MyReadingLab course. Your instructor already has your COURSEID, so make sure you have that before logging in.

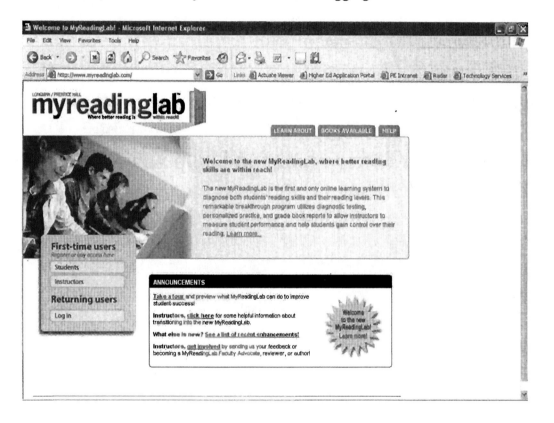

2) Click on "Students" under "First-Time Users." Here you will be prompted to enter your access code, enter your e-mail address, and choose your own Login Name and Password. **Once you register, you can click on "Returning Users" and use your new login name and password every time you go back into your course in MyReadingLab.**

After logging in, you will see all the ways MyReadingLab can help you become a better reader.

www.myreadinglab.com

HOME PAGE ...

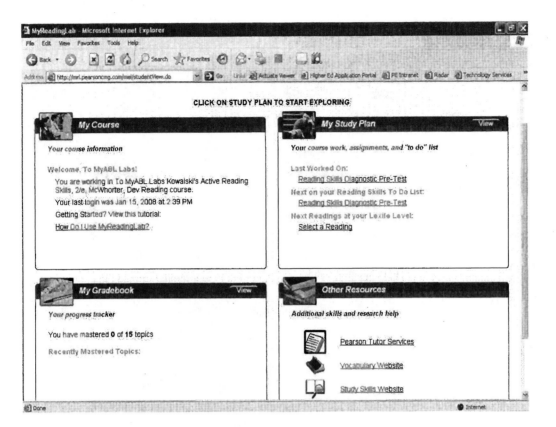

Here is your MyReadingLab Home Page. You get a quick summary of your course standing(s) every time you log in.

Your course box displays the class details. Your Study Plan box shows what you last worked on and what is next on your To Do list.

Your Gradebook box shows you how many topics you have mastered in the class.

Your Other Resources box supplies you with amazing tools such as:

- Pearson Tutor Services – click here and see how you can get help on your papers by qualified tutors ... before handing them in!
- Vocabulary Website – this site provides additional support with definitions of key words, quizzes, and more to help you develop your vocabulary skills.
- Study Skills – extra help that includes tips, and quizzes on how to improve your study skills.
- Research Navigator – click here and see how this resembles your library with access to online journals to research paper assignments.

Now, let's start practicing to become better readers. Click on the Study Plan tab. This is where you will do all your course work.

www.myreadinglab.com

STUDY PLAN …

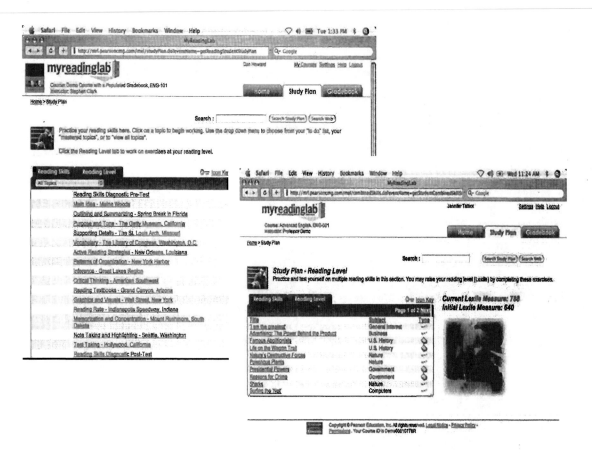

The extensive practice in *MyReadingLab* was designed to make you a better reader. Practice opportunities come in two formats:

- practice with the individual skills to improve you **reading skill** mastery.
- practice reading comprehension skills to improve your **reading level.** Your instructor can choose to offer this section to you, so you may or may not see this in your MyReadingLab course.

MyReadingLab allows you to practice reading skills through a mastery-based format in which you get an overview of the skill, see models of the skill at work, go through an abundance of practice exercises to apply what you have learned, and then take a mastery test.

www.myreadinglab.com

DIAGNOSTIC PRE-TESTS ...

Your instructor may assign the Reading Skill diagnostic pre-test to assess your strengths at the individual skill level. The Reading Level diagnostic provides you with an initial "Lexile" measurement, which you and your instructor can use to measure reading level progress through the semester.

After completing the diagnostic pre-test, you can return to your study plan and work on any concepts that you have yet to master.

www.myreadinglab.com

GRADEBOOK ...

Let's look at how your MyReadingLab gradebook will help you track your progress.

Click on the "Gradebook" tab and the "Student Detail" report

Here you are able to see how you are doing in each area. If you feel you need to go back and review, simply click on any score and your score sheet will appear.

You also have a Diagnostic Detail report so you can go back and review your diagnostic pretest and see how much MyReadingLab has helped you improve!

HERE TO HELP YOU ...

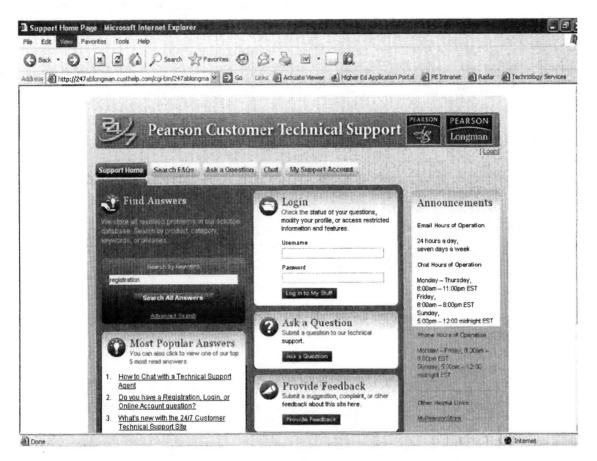

Our goal is to provide answers to your MyReadingLab questions as quickly as possible and deliver the highest level of support. By visiting www.myreadinglab.com/help.html, many questions can be resolved in just a few minutes or less. Here you will find help on:

- System Requirements
- How to Register for MyReadingLab
- How to Use MyReadingLab

Contact Support. We also invite you to contact Pearson Product Support (above). You can contact our Support Representatives online at http://247.pearsoned.com. Here you can:

- Search Frequently Asked Questions about MyReadingLab
- E-mail a Question to our Support Team
- Chat with a Support Representative

MySkillsLab 2.0 (www.myskillslab.com)
This exciting website houses all the media tools any developmental English student will need to improve their reading, writing, and study skills, and all in one easy to use place.

The Longman Vocabulary Web Site (*http://www.ablongman.com/vocabulary*)
This unique website features hundreds of exercises in ten topic areas to strengthen vocabulary skills. Students will also benefit from "100 Words That All High School Graduates Should Know," a useful resource that provides definitions for each of the words on this list, vocabulary flashcards and audio clips to help facilitate pronunciation skills. *Open access.*

Longman Study Skills Website (http://www.ablongman.com/studyskills) This site offers hundreds of review strategies for college success, time and stress management skills, study strategies, and more. Students can take a variety of assessment tests to learn about their organizational skills and learning styles, with follow-up quizzes to reinforce the strategies they have learned. *Open access.*

Q: Are your students required to pass a state exam?

STATE SPECIFIC SUPPLEMENTS

<u>For Florida Adopters:</u>

Thinking Through the Test: A Study Guide for the Florida College Basic Skills Exit Test
D.J. Henry / Mimi Markus

This workbook helps students strengthen their reading and/or writing skills in preparation for the Florida College Basic Skills Exit Test. It features both diagnostic tests to help assess areas that may need improvement and exit tests to help test skill mastery. Detailed explanatory answers have been provided for almost all of the questions. Package item only—not available for sale.

An excellent study tool for students preparing to take Florida College Basic Skills Exit Test for Reading, this laminated reading grid summarizes all the skills tested on the Exit Exam. Package item only—not available for sale.

Available Versions:

Thinking Through the Test: A Study Guide for the Florida College Basic Skills Tests, Reading (with Answer Key), 3/e	(0-321-38737-6)
Thinking Through the Test: A Study Guide for the Florida College Basic Skills Tests, Reading (without Answer Key), 3/E	(0-321-38738-4)
Thinking Summary for the Florida State Exit Exam by D.J. Henry	(0-321-08478-0)

The Florida Exit Test Study Guide for Reading (0-13-184899-2)
Designed specifically for students preparing for the Florida Exit Test, this study guide provides instruction and practice on the individual skills covered and also provides one complete sample test.

Reading Skills Summary for the Florida State Exit Exam, by D. J. Henry (0-321-08478-0)
An excellent study tool for students preparing to take Florida College Basic Skills Exit Test for Reading, this laminated reading grid summarizes all the skills tested on the Exit Exam.

<u>For Texas Adopters</u>

The Longman THEA Study Guide by Jeanette Harris (0-321-27240-0)
Created specifically for students in Texas, this study guide includes straightforward explanations and numerous practice exercises to help students prepare for the reading and writing sections of THEA Test. Package item only--not available for sale.

The Prentice Hall THEA Study Guide for Reading (0-13-183643-9)
Designed specifically for students preparing for Texas Higher Education Assessment, this study guide provides instruction and practice on the individual skills and also provides one complete sample test.

For New York/CUNY Adopters

For New York/CUNY Adopters
Preparing for the CUNY-ACT Reading and Writing Test edited by Patricia Licklider (0-321-19608-2)
This booklet, prepared by reading and writing faculty from across the CUNY system, is designed to help students prepare for the CUNY-ACT exit test. It includes test-taking tips, reading passages, typical exam questions, and sample writing prompts to help students become familiar with each portion of the test.

Developmental Reading Instructor Resources

Printed Test Bank for Developmental Reading (0-321-08596-5)
Offers more than 3,000 questions in all areas of reading, including vocabulary, main idea, supporting details, patterns of organization, critical thinking, analytical reasoning, inference, point of view, visual aides, and textbook reading. (Electronic also available; see CDs)

Electronic Test Bank for Developmental Reading (0-321-08179-X)
Offers more than 3,000 questions in all areas of reading, including vocabulary, main idea, supporting details, patterns of organization, critical thinking, analytical reasoning, inference, point of view, visual aides, and textbook reading. Instructors simply choose questions, then print out the completed test for distribution OR offer the test online.

The Prentice Hall Reading Skills Test Bank (0-13-041249-X)
This test bank contains 1,100 exercises, covering word analysis, context clues, stated main idea, implied main idea, tone and bias, details, major vs. minor details, style, study reading, reading rate, and visual aids. Questions are multiple-choice, matching, or true/false. Available in print only.

STATE SUPPLEMENTS
CLAST Test Package, 4/e (0-321-01950-4)
These two, 40-item objective tests evaluate students' readiness for the Florida CLAST exams. Strategies for teaching CLAST preparedness are included.

COVERAGE FOR THE THEA AND CLAST READING SKILLS PROFICIENCY TESTS

College students in many states are required to demonstrate proficiency on reading tests that include a variety of skills. The following list shows where the skills on two such tests, the THEA and the CLAST, are covered in *Breaking Through*.

General Test Taking Skills   Chapter 7

THEA (Texas Higher Education Assessment)

Determine the meaning of words and phrases
Context clues   Chapter 3
Multiple meanings   Chapter 3
Figurative language   Chapter 10

Understand main ideas and supporting details
Explicit or stated main idea   Chapter 4
Implicit or implied main idea   Chapter 4
Recognizing supporting details   Chapter 5

Identify a writer's purpose, point of view, and intended meaning   Chapter 11

Analyze relationship among ideas
Organizational patterns   Chapter 5
Drawing conclusions   Chapter 10, 11

Use critical reading skills to evaluate written material
Stated and implied assumptions   Chapter 10
Fact and opinion   Chapter 11
Logic   Chapter 9
Validity of analogies   Chapter 3
Bias of writer   Chapter 11

Apply study skills

CLAST (Florida College Level Academic Skills Test)

Literal Comprehension

Critical Comprehension Skills

Instructor Resource Center

Getting Registered

To register for the Instructor Resource Center, go to www.pearsonhighered.com and click **"Educators"**.

1. Click **"Download teaching resources for your text"** in the blue welcome box.
2. Request access to download digital supplements by clicking the **"Request Access"** link.

Follow the provided instructions. Once you have been verified as a valid Pearson instructor, an instructor code will be emailed to you. Please use this code to set up your Pearson login name and password. After you have set up

----

Downloading Resources

1. Go to http://www.pearsonhighered.com/educator and use the "Search our catalog" option to find your text. You may search by Author, Title, or ISBN.

----

2. **Select your text** from the provided results.

> **Title**
> **Writing for Life: Paragraph to Essay (with MyWritingLab), 1/e**
> **Henry**
> ©2008 | Longman | Paper Bound with PIN; 736 pp | Out of Stock
> ISBN-10: 0205574580 | ISBN-13: 9780205574582

----

3. After being directed to the catalog page for your text, click the **Instructor Resources** link located under the **Resources** tab.

Clicking the Instructor Resources link will provide a list of all of the book-specific print and digital resources for your text below the main title. Items available for download will have a 🔲 icon.

----

4. **Click on the View Downloadable Files** link next to the resource you want to download.

> View Downloadable Files

A pop-up box will appear showing which files you have selected to download. Once you select the files, you will be prompted to login with an Instructor Resource Center login.

----

5. Enter your login name and password, and click the **"Submit"** button.

----

6. Read the terms and conditions and then click the **"I accept"** button to begin the download process.

> I accept (proceed with download)

> Cancel (closes this window)

7. **"Save"** the supplement file to a folder you can easily find again.

Once you are signed into the IRC, you may continue to download additional resources from our online catalog.

Please "Sign Out" when you are finished.

To Reach the Authors

If you have comments, suggestions, or need more information, call Brenda at 404-233-1116 or LeeAnn at 281-478-2770. We would like to hear from you.

Brenda D. Smith and LeeAnn Morris

Chapter One

Student Success

Success begins with a positive attitude and with the belief that success is attainable. Students of college reading usually need a little "pep talk" at the beginning of the course. Many come with a negative feeling about being there. They know they have failed to meet college reading requirements and are upset with themselves for having to take a developmental course.

Chapter Objectives:
- Are you a winner?
- Do you think about what you "can do" or what you "cannot"?
- Do you set high standards?
- Do you plan for success?
- How can you manage time efficiently?
- What are the behaviors of success?
- How can fellow students be learning resources?
- What student responsibilities determine success in college?

Transparency Masters:
1.1   Reader's Tips: *Time Savers* and *Making a Learning Schedule*
1.2   Reader's Tips: *Limiting Your Net Search* and *Using Institutional Indexes*

Suggested Teaching Activities:
1.   An instructor can help improve students' attitudes and self-images by talking about goal setting and relating success stories. Use the video *Famous Failures* (http://www.youtube.com/watch?v=Y6hz_s2XIAU) to illustrate how people such as Michael Jordan, Lucille Ball, Walt Disney, and others were met with a great deal of adversity and examine what made them persevere.

2.	Talk about short-term and long-term goals and ask students to answer the following questions:

- What are my goals for the next six months?
- What activities will help me achieve these goals?
- What is the best use of my time right now?

3.	Use the Goal Setting Worksheet handout that follows to help students develop the habit of setting short term goals regularly.

4.	To achieve success, students must be willing to sacrifice. Sacrifice is more strictly defined for some than for others. Discuss the obvious sacrifices of time and money, and then move to the not-so-obvious everyday sacrifices, like not talking on the telephone or not watching that additional TV show, that will make a difference in the long run.

5.	As a teaching strategy, encourage students to visit a freshman lecture class and to take notes on both the lecture and the behavior of other students. Talk about the choices that students make. Discuss the possible consequences of behavior such as missing class, arriving late, sleeping in class, and not taking notes. Ask students to predict the A and B students from their class observations and to explain their predictions.

6.	Help students learn their campus and about college in general by having them complete a campus scavenger hunt. This is a fun activity to do with a partner. A sample campus scavenger hunt is included here and is easy enough to modify to your particular campus.

7.	While time consuming, personal conferences with students in your office have huge dividends. Not only do students learn where your office is, they enjoy talking about themselves, and many students begin to feel more comfortable with you as an authority figure.

8.	Explain to students that research says the sooner they declare a major and get on a career path, the more likely they are to complete their degree. Invite a career counselor in to explain the significance of a degree plan and how to go about setting one up.

9.	As an exercise to improve self-image, ask the students to list ten interesting things about themselves. Then ask them to share the list with a classmate and have each write a statement to introduce the other to the class. To vary this activity, have each student use an overhead for outlining the information when introducing a classmate.

10.	You may want to suggest that students do outside reading on self-improvement. Such books tend to be easy to read and motivating. Many students have never been exposed to positive mental attitude books and find them quite inspiring. You may want to suggest some titles, although most students like to browse in a store and pick their own.

11.	Work with students on time management, and explain how it relates to college success and business success. Reinforce the use of time charts by asking students to complete a semester calendar in addition to weekly ones. Students may choose to use a personal planner, but I have found it more effective to have students keep weekly calendars in their notebooks that are checked during the semester. A generic weekly planner is included here.

12.	Interaction and personal reflection are goals for students reading the selections in Chapter One. The questions at the end of the readings have no correct answers. The aim is to have students bring a part of themselves to the print and to allow themselves to be affected by the message. The following questions, which may be used either before or after reading, may help guide your discussion of each selection.

Think Success

Does success begin as an attitude?
Why do some people achieve more than others?

Plan for Success

Do you manage your time, or does your time manage you?
How can you get control of your day?

Act Successful

What makes people look successful?
How does a successful student act?
How do you act successful?

Networking

What is collaborative learning?
Is it wrong to study together?
What bonds students to their educational institution? Is it athletics, clubs, or academics?
Why do businesspeople network?

Personal Feedback

Use the Personal Feedback sections to help you learn about your students and to help them learn about themselves. Shared information promotes bonding, which leads to your becoming a "significant other" adult on that student's success team. Ask students to use the perforations to turn the feedback pages in to you. You may want to give 5 to 10 points credit for each completed feedback sheet.

Incorporating MRL: Guide students to the Pearson Study Skills website in MRL and have them work through the activities and resources in the Getting Started section of the website.

Reading Workshop Tip: As an initial reading journal assignment, have students write about their personal reading. Pose questions regarding reading attitudes, favorite books and authors, their reading history, etc.

Name: _____   Week of _____

Weekly Goals

I.   Last week's goals: Review the goal you set for yourself last week and complete or respond to the following statements:

A.   My personal goal for last week was _____.

B.   Did I reach that goal? (circle one)   Yes   No

C.   I was able to accomplish my goal because

_____

_____.

OR

I was unable to accomplish my goal because

_____

_____.

II.   This week's goals: Think about what you would like to accomplish this week.

A.   List two or three things you want to accomplish this week. At least one goal must be school related.

1)

2)

3)

B.   Choose one of the goals from A and complete the following:

1)   Specific Goal:

_____

2)   Target Date and Time: _____

3)   Steps necessary to complete this goal: _____

_____

Reward: _____

4

Name _____

	Sun	Mon	Tue	Wed	Thu	Fri	Sat
7:00							
:30							
8:00							
:30							
9:00							
:30							
10:00							
:30							
11:00							
:30							
12:00							
:30							
1:00							
:30							
2:00							
:30							
3:00							
:30							
4:00							
:30							
5:00							
:30							
6:00							
:30							
7:00							
:30							
8:00							
:30							
9:00							

WHO, WHAT, WHERE ON CAMPUS?

DIRECTIONS: College life is much easier and fuller when you know what your college offers and where. This activity will help you become better acquainted with your school. All questions can be answered by touring the campus and using current publications such as the <u>Catalog of Courses</u>, <u>Student Handbook</u>, and <u>Schedule of Classes</u>.

1. Find your professor's office. Have him/her initial this sheet (probably during your conference.)

2. What is the name of the library? What color is the floor at the circulation desk?

3. What document/s must you have to check out materials from the library? What are the weekend hours this semester?

4. How many computers are available in the Electronic Resources area of the library? List two data bases you can access from these computers.

5. Where is the Financial Aid Office? What is the application deadline for next semester?

6. What is the primary federal grant available for students who need financial aid?

7. Is child care available on campus? If so, for what ages?

8. What menu item from the cafeteria looks most appealing to you? Price?

9. When does the bookstore buy back books during the current semester?

10. What is the police department's non-emergency number?

11. What is the campus emergency number that can be dialed from any extension on campus?

12. List two student organizations you might consider joining.

13. In what office can you get more information about student organizations? Where is it?

14. Where is the campus billiards room, and what is it called?

15. Where is the campus post office? Its windows face which direction?

16. Where is the Employment/Career Office located? List two of their services.

17. Where can you use a computer to type and print a paper for a class? Can you set up an e-mail account there?

18. Write the full name of the A.A. and A.A.S. degrees.

19 List one college degree or certificate program that interests you and the document and page number that describes the requirements.

20. What is the name of the college newspaper?

21. When is your last final exam this semester? (date, time, course number)

23 What is the penalty for cheating/plagiarism?

24. What reading skill level is required to take American History Before 1877?

25. What are the professor's name, office location and phone number for the hardest class you have this semester?

Reader's Tip
Time Savers

Using time wisely becomes a habit. Analyze your current problems according to the following principles of time management to gain greater control of yourself and your environment.

1. Plan. Keep an appointment book by the day and hour. Write a daily To Do List.
2. Start with the most critical activity of the day and work your way down to the least important one.
3. Ask yourself, "What is the best use of my time right now?"
4. Don't do what doesn't need doing.
5. Concentrate completely on one thing at a time.
6. Block out big chunks of time for large projects.
7. Make use of five-, ten-, and fifteen-minute segments of time.
8. Keep phone calls short or avoid them.
9. Listen well for clear instructions.
10. Learn to say "No!" to yourself and others.
11. Limit your TV, video game, and text messaging time.
12. Strive for excellence, but realize that perfection may not be worth the cost.

Reader's Tip
Making a Learning Schedule

Use your assignment calendar to devise a learning schedule. Mark important dates for this class.

- Enter all test dates and due dates for papers and projects.
- Divide reading assignments into manageable units and record as daily and weekly goals. Leave several days for study and review before tests.
- Record dates for completing extra library and Internet readings.
- Analyze assigned projects and create daily or weekly goals. Record start dates and interim small step goals.
- Designate dates for completing the first draft of written reports.
- Use your calendar of expected achievements to stay on schedule in each of your classes.

Reader's Tip
Limiting Your Net Search

- Enter **"AND"** or a **+** sign between each word of your search. For example, using the words *Apple Computer* for your search will turn up thousands of hits that include not only sites about the company, but also sites related to apple (the fruit) and sites about computers in general. Using *AND* in your key phrase (*Apple AND Computer*) will return sites that only contain both words in the phrase.
- Enter **"OR"** to broaden a search. *Apple OR Computer* will return sites that contain information about either apples or computers.
- Enter **"NOT"** to exclude items. *Apple AND Computer NOT fruit* will exclude sites that mention fruit and computers.
- Use quotation marks when you want only hits that contain the exact phrase, such as "Apple Computer Financial Report for 2001."

Reader's Tip
Using Institutional Indexes

Indexes are *databases* that categorize articles according to topics for easy access. Check with your library for the following popular college databases, which are paid for by your institution. Your college's web site might have a direct link to the library's holdings.

Galileo
Periodical Abstracts
Newspaper Abstracts
Lexis-Nexis Academic Universe
MLA Bibliography
ABI Inform
PsycFIRST
Social Science Abstracts
ERIC
MEDLINE

Stages of Reading

Students think of reading as having only one stage, the "during" stage. The goal of Chapter Two is to help students see that reading is an interactive, three-stage process in which they use prior knowledge in all three stages to construct meaning. Stress the importance of activating schemata and adding to the "computer chips" by being a model for your students through pre-reading and post-reading activities.

Chapter Objectives:
- What is reading?
- What is "knowing about knowing"?
- What is schema?
- What do good readers think about as they read?
- How can you remember what you read?

Transparency Masters:
2.1   Stages of Reading
2.2   Six Thinking Strategies of Good Readers
2.3   Reader's Tips: *Questions for Previewing* and *React and Reflect*
2.4   Reader's Tips: *Reading and Studying Health* and *Reading and Studying Science*
2.5   Reader's Tip: *Reading and Studying Criminal Justice*
2.6   Reader's Tips: *Reading a News Story* and *Reading a Feature Story*

Suggested teaching activities:
1.   To gain metacognitive control, students need to know what good readers do. Do not just tell them. Research indicates that you must show them the six thinking strategies of good readers in order to see an improvement. Model these skills for your students. Many materials are appropriate for demonstrating, but particularly useful materials are the *Reading for*

Understanding (RFU) cards by *Science Research Associates (SRA)*. These cards have been around for a long time, but they are very well done. In modeling your own thinking as an expert reader on these short, two- or three-sentence items, you can show how all six strategies are used to make meaning.

2.   Reading recall is difficult to command. It can be requested, but the demand may be overlooked and is rarely accomplished. To encourage recall, explain the importance of recitation and encourage students to connect the new information with the old and to evaluate its worth.

3.   Ask students if they are "buying in" or "tuning out" after reading. The reaction or evaluation stage may be done subconsciously or not done at all. Help students to be aware of the need to react to text.

4.   Give each student a bookmark which will serve as a constant reminder of the reading process. Use the template on the following page to print bookmarks on tag board.

Incorporating MRL: Direct students to the Reading Textbooks module in MRL. Here they can practice previewing textbooks and chapters.

Reading Workshop Tip: If students are having difficulty selecting a book to read on their own, have them think about the types of movies they enjoy. Then, lead them to a Web site such as www.amazon.com or www.audible.com and suggest they browse through the genres. They can read a brief synopsis of any book they may be interested in as well as reviews and ratings of those books.

COMPREHENSION TIPS

Before Reading
PREVIEW:
Read title,
Introduction,
Headings,
Subheadings,
Special print
Visual aids,
Summary
SET GOALS
ACTIVATE SCHEMA

During Reading
INTEGRATE
KNOWLEDGE
Predict
Picture
Relate
Monitor
Correct
Reread
Read on
Change
predictions
Seek help
Annotate (mark
text)

After Reading
RECALL
Talk about it
Write about it
In a journal
Make notes
Summarize
REACT
Evaluate

L. Morris

COMPREHENSION TIPS

Before Reading
PREVIEW:
Read title,
Introduction,
Headings,
Subheadings,
Special print
Visual aids,
Summary
SET GOALS
ACTIVATE SCHEMA

During Reading
INTEGRATE
KNOWLEDGE
Predict
Picture
Relate
Monitor
Correct
Reread
Read on
Change
predictions
Seek help
Annotate (mark
text)

After Reading
RECALL
Talk about it
Write about it
In a journal
Make notes
Summarize
REACT
Evaluate

L. Morris

COMPREHENSION TIPS

Before Reading
PREVIEW:
Read title,
Introduction,
Headings,
Subheadings,
Special print
Visual aids,
Summary
SET GOALS
ACTIVATE SCHEMA

During Reading
INTEGRATE
KNOWLEDGE
Predict
Picture
Relate
Monitor
Correct
Reread
Read on
Change
predictions
Seek help
Annotate (mark
text)

After Reading
RECALL
Talk about it
Write about it
In a journal
Make notes
Summarize
REACT
Evaluate

L. Morris

COMPREHENSION TIPS

Before Reading
PREVIEW:
Read title,
Introduction,
Headings,
Subheadings,
Special print
Visual aids,
Summary
SET GOALS
ACTIVATE SCHEMA

During Reading
INTEGRATE
KNOWLEDGE
Predict
Picture
Relate
Monitor
Correct
Reread
Read on
Change
predictions
Seek help
Annotate (mark
text)

After Reading
RECALL
Talk about it
Write about it
In a journal
Make notes
Summarize
REACT
Evaluate

L. Morris

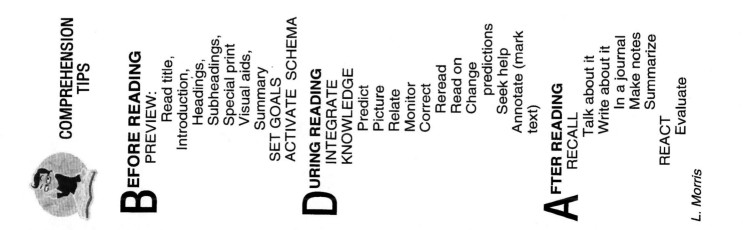

STAGES OF READING

Before

- Preview
- Set Goals
- Activate Schema

During

- Predict
- Picture
- Relate
- Monitor
- Correct
- Annotate

After

- Recall
- React

SIX THINKING STRATEGIES OF GOOD READERS

1. Predict

Make Educated Guesses

2. Picture

Form Images

3. Relate

Draw Comparisons

4. Monitor

Check Understanding

5. Resolve Gaps in Understanding

Seek Solutions to Confusion

6. Annotate:

Circle, Underline, and Write Brief Marginal Notes

SELECTION 1: IMPROVED EATING FOR THE COLLEGE STUDENT

Answer with T (true) or F (false).

Comprehension Quiz (for prereading or postreading)

F   _____   1. Fast foods tend to be high in fat but low in sodium.

T   _____   2. Most fast-food chains have nutritional analyses of menu items.

F   _____   3. To eat healthfully, it is not necessary to avoid fried foods.

F   _____   4. According to the reading, a large percentage of adults experience food allergies.

T   _____   5. Food allergies can result in rashes or a severe swelling of the tongue.

F   _____   6. For children, one of the food allergens that cause the most problems is garden peas.

T   _____   7. Organic foods are reported to be pesticide- and chemical-free.

F   _____   8. The author recommends eating organic food even though the cost is higher.

T   _____   9. Antioxidants produce enzymes that destroy excess free radicals.

Vocabulary Quiz (for prereading or postreading)

T   _____   1. Wild animals *forage* for food in the forest.

F   _____   2. When buying a new car, money is not usually a *constraint* in choosing options.

T   _____   3. Movie stars often feel they are *maligned* by articles in tabloid papers.

F   _____   4. A vegetarian would tend not to be a *discriminating* eater.

T   _____   5. Cooking with *lard* adds calories that tend not to be nutritious.

T   _____   6. If you *opt* for every summer school session, you can accelerate your graduation.

T   _____   7. *Intolerance* promotes hate rather than acceptance.

T   _____   8. For allergy sufferers, spring pollen can *trigger* sinus problems.

T   _____   9. A manager who completes a job early and under budget could possibly receive a *hefty* bonus.

F   _____   10. The view of a junkyard is considered *pristine* by most observers.

SELECTION 2:   THE GALVESTON DISASTER

Answer with T *(true) or* F *(false).*

Comprehension Quiz (for prereading or postreading)

T   _____   1. The greatest natural disaster to strike the U.S. was the tropical cyclone that hit Galveston, Texas in 1900.

T   _____   2. Galveston is located on an island off the Texas coast.

F   _____   3. Even though they had the means to do so, weather forecasters failed to warn the public of the coming storm.

F   _____   4. Residents of Galveston could not escape the storm because of massive traffic jams and accidents on the exit bridges.

T   _____   5. During reconstruction of Galveston, a high sea wall was built for protection against another possible disaster.

T   _____   6. Dr. Isaac Cline gave a late warning for the storm's danger.

F   _____   7. A steamship was used to evacuate Galveston residents.

T   _____   8. The storm surge hit at high tide.

F   _____   9. Only two feet of water covered the highest point in Galveston during the height of the storm.

F   _____   10. Since the historic storm, Galveston has suffered three other major hurricanes of similar force.

Vocabulary Quiz (for prereading or postreading)

T   _____   1. If *fatalities* are related to a robbery, murder charges could follow.

F   _____   2. A *barrier island* is always without vegetation.

F   _____   3. If the crime scene is *amiss*, the area is orderly and predictable.

T   _____   4. On the day after Thanksgiving, shoppers *flock* to stores for bargains.

F   _____   5. To *gawk* at a poorly dressed passerby is a polite reaction.

F   _____   6. An *imminent* event is scheduled for the far distance future.

F   _____   7. If the stock market *plummeted*, investors probably celebrated their profits.

T   _____   8. The *flotsam* in a bay can be seaweed or beer cans.

T   _____   9. Canals are *dredged* so that boats can pass.

F   _____   10. Water with *sediment* is desirable for drinking.

SELECTION 3: WAS ERIC CLARK INSANE OR JUST TROUBLED?

Answer with T *(true) or* F *(false).*

Comprehension Quiz (for prereading or postreading)

F _____ 1. Terry Clark correctly assumed her son Gentry was the prime suspect.

T _____ 2. Eric Clark was a star football player and did well in school.

T _____ 3. Eric Clark suffered from schizophrenia.

F _____ 4. Eric Clark was charged with 'guilty except insane.'

T _____ 5. Eric Clark's case was the first constitutional challenge to the insanity defense since new restrictions were imposed.

T _____ 6. One of the early signs of Eric's illness was his loss of interest in sports.

T _____ 7. Terry Clark decided her son was schizophrenic when he called his parents aliens.

T _____ 8. Some people feel that Arizona law violates a mentally ill person's right to a fair trial.

F _____ 9. Eric Clark's father was a practicing psychologist.

T _____ 10. Terry Clark wants her son imprisoned only if he receives treatment for his illness.

Vocabulary Quiz (for prereading or postreading)

T _____ 1. The assembly ended *abruptly* after the speaker was interrupted.

F _____ 2. A person who is found mentally *competent* does not have to stand trial.

T _____ 3. The inmate's *incarceration* was spent in total isolation.

F _____ 4. The accused mayor's *acquittal* meant he would stand trial for embezzling funds.

T _____ 5. In his opening remarks, the judge *alluded* to what his decision would be.

F _____ 6. *Schizophrenia* is not considered a form of mental illness.

T _____ 7. The investigators quickly *surmised* that the burglar had left the residence before they arrived.

T _____ 8. The *severity* of plagiarism may get a student expelled from school.

T _____ 9. Kara's performance in the play *took a dive* after her illness.

T _____ 10. Juan's *psychosis* was difficult for his doctors to diagnose.

Reader's Tip
Questions for Previewing

Use the following questions as guides to energize your reading and help you become an active learner:

1. What is the topic of the material?
2. What do I already know about the subject?
3. What is my purpose for reading?
4. How is the material organized?
5. What will be my plan of attack?

Reader's Tip
React and Reflect

After recalling what an author has said, evaluate its significance for you by answering the following questions:

- Did I enjoy the reading? Why or why not?
- Was the selection well-written? Explain specifics.
- Do I agree or disagree with the author? Why or why not?
- How many of the author's ideas do I accept?

Reader's Tip
Reading and Studying Health

- Use learning aids provided within the text. Such items might include running glossaries on pages, checklists, discussion and application questions, and summaries.
- Answer any marginal questions placed within a chapter.
- Review and understand procedures by following the graphics provided.
- Design your own concept cards to help learn new vocabulary.
- Draw simple figures or symbols to aid your understanding and recall of concepts.

Reader's Tip
Reading and Studying Science

- Master a concept by explaining it in your own words.
- Draw your own scientific models and diagram the processes to reinforce learning them.
- Use illustrations as a reading and review tool before exams.
- Use chapter summaries as study checklists to be sure you have reviewed all the chapter material.
- Think like a scientist at the textbook Web site by participating in virtual research activities.
- Use mnemonics to memorize. Remember the example **M**any **P**eople **F**ind **P**arachuting **A**larming to remember the five kingdoms, which are monera, protista, fungi, plantae, and animalia.
- Know the theories you are applying in lab and their significance.
- Blend lecture, lab, and textbook notes.

Reader's Tip
Reading and Studying Criminal Justice

- Identify criminal acts in legal terms. Make lists to commit to memory.
- Distinguish between the types of crimes and categories of criminals. Use charts to form groups.
- Know the legal behaviors and responsibilities required for making an arrest and gathering evidence. Make timelines.
- Understand the processes of the courts and the sequencing of legal actions. Create a flowchart for a visual display.
- Relate possible legal decisions and police actions to the balance of police powers and democratic freedoms.

Reader's Tip
Reading a News Story

- ***Get an overview from the headline and photographs.***
- Answer the 5 W's and the H.
    - **Who** is the story about?
    - **What** happened?
    - **When** did it happen?
    - **Where** did the event or events take place?
    - **Why** did this event occur?
    - **How** did this happen?
- Continue to read according to the amount of detail desired.

Reader's Tip
Reading a Feature Story

- How does the angle or focus of a feature story differ from that of a straight news story?
- How credible are the sources cited?
- Is it factual or sensationalized?
- Does the reporter show a bias?
- Does the reporter judge or do you decide?

CHAPTER 2 VOCABULARY LESSON QUIZ

Part I: Indicate whether the following sentences are True (T) or False (F).

F _____ 1. When the weather is *intolerably* hot, people usually wear heavy coats.

F _____ 2. A person with an *insatiable* appetite is usually satisfied after a small meal.

F _____ 3. When troops are *disarmed*, they are provided with more advanced weaponry for fighting.

T _____ 4. When someone is *inaccessible*, he or she cannot be easily reached.

F _____ 5. The *unabridged* versions of classic novels can be found in "Cliffs Notes" that summarize the message.

F _____ 6. An *inhospitable* environment is warm and inviting.

F _____ 7. If you are dedicated to comparison shopping, you feel it is *improbable* that you will find a better deal than your first price.

T _____ 8. Because the millionaire's will made it clear that the child had been *disinherited*, the child received nothing.

T _____ 9. A person who *disregards* speed limits is more likely to receive a speeding ticket than a person who adheres rigorously to them.

T _____ 10. Weary travelers are generally *disconcerted* when they miss connecting flights.

Part II: Choose the best word from the list as an antonym for the following words in italics.

available	entrust	commendable	mortal	activate
changed	coagulate	abundant	tranquil	praise

_____ 11. Sugar will quickly *dissolve* into hot tea to make "sweet tea."

_____ 12. Greek and Roman gods were said to be *immortal,* and thus they had no fear of death.

_____ 13. While many music critics *discredited* the lyrical content of the song, it pleased many listeners.

_____ 14. Despite the supervisor's aura of being *untouchable*, he was quite receptive to meeting with his employees.

_____ 15. The developers were unable to complete construction of the shopping center due to *inadequate* funds.

_____ 16. He was *immobilized* as a result of his injuries, and was restricted to bed rest.

_____ 17. Parents do not generally respect *disgraceful* activities.

_____ 18. The wedding dress fit the bride perfectly, even though it was *unaltered.*

_____ 19. Due to the *inclement* weather, the children were not allowed to go outside for recess.

_____ 20. After several laptops were reported missing, there was an atmosphere that made you *distrust* others in the office.

11. coagulate 12. mortal 13. praise 14. available 15. abundant
16. activate 17. commendable 18. changed 19. tranquil 20. entrust

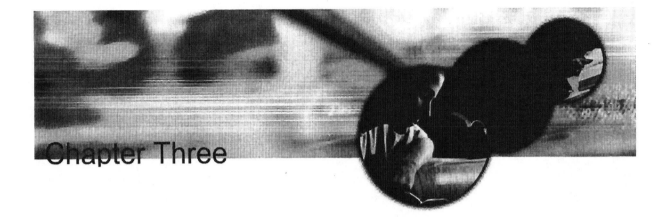

Chapter Three

Vocabulary

We can force students to memorize words for a test, but how can we help them remember the new words forever? Ideally, students should be immersed in a whole new environment where they hear the words used frequently. This is how young children learn language. Realistically, we can't transplant our students, but we can talk about the new words and try to use them as often as possible.

Chapter Objectives:
- What are context clues?
- What are roots, prefixes, and suffixes?
- How do you use the dictionary?
- Do words have "families"?
- What is a glossary?
- Why use a thesaurus?
- What comparisons form analogies?

Transparency Masters
3.1   Unlocking Word Meaning
3.2   Reader's Tips: *Using an Electronic Thesaurus* and *Categories of Relationships for Analogies*
3.3   Reader's Tip: *Easily Confused Words*
3.4   Multiple Meaning Mix

Suggested Teaching Activities:
1.   Encourage students to use concept cards. As you will discover, some words are more appropriate than others for concept cards. However, even for a word like *transmit*, which can easily be remembered structurally by prefix and root, the card and a picture will form additional links to aid student memory.

23

Demonstrate how the concept cards can be made. Suggest a word, discuss its meaning and use, and ask students for vivid visualizations. Help them arrive at a phrase and an image that suggest the meaning of a word. The creative part is particularly difficult for some students. For class discussion, you may want to try the following phrases:

extinct animal

deceptive answer

prestigious address

2.   Guide students to Web sites such as www.flashcards.com where they can create, and print if desired, customizable flashcards.

3.   As you know, context clues and structural analysis are two effective strategies for unlocking meaning in unknown words. Provide students with opportunities to practice unlocking meaning to unknown words they encounter using context clues and word structure on the following charts. Give them these simple instructions:

Context Strategy:

Follow these steps to unlocking the meanings of unfamiliar words through context clues:

1. As you encounter an unfamiliar word, record it in the Unfamiliar Word column.

2. Now look at the rest of the sentence and surrounding sentences. Try to locate words and phrases that hint at the meaning of the unfamiliar word. Record these words or phrases in the Hints/Clues column.

3. Using the hints and clues, predict a meaning for the word and jot it in the Predicted Meaning column. With practice, your predictions should become more accurate.

4. Finally, look up the word in a dictionary, locate the definition that seems to most accurately fit the context of the sentence and record it in the Dictionary Meaning column. Compare your predicted definition with the dictionary definition.

Word Structure Analysis Strategy:

1. As you encounter an unfamiliar word in your reading, record it in the Unfamiliar Word column.

2. Now examine the word for any word parts that you recognize and write them in the Word Part column. Next, write the meanings of those word parts. Combine your knowledge of the word parts with the context of the sentence and write a Predicted Meaning. Last, look the new word up in a dictionary and record the definition on the chart. Compare your predicted meaning with the dictionary meaning.

Incorporating MRL: As students work through the MRL modules, encourage them to keep a log of unfamiliar words that they may want to spend some time with later. Provide students with copies of the vocabulary charts (on the following pages) for unlocking new meanings through structural analysis and context clues.

Reading Workshop Tip: Just as you encouraged students to keep a log of unfamiliar words when working in My Reading Lab, this is an especially good tip for students to use while reading their novels as well.

Vocabulary Enrichment
Context Strategy

Unfamiliar Word	Hints / Clues	Predicted Meaning	Dictionary Meaning

Vocabulary Enrichment
Structural Analysis Strategy

Unfamiliar Word	Word Part	Meaning of Word Part	Predicted Meaning	Dictionary Meaning

UNLOCKING WORD MEANING

Context Clues
- Definition
- Elaborating Details
- Elaborating Examples
- Comparison
- Contrast

Word Parts
- Roots
- Prefixes
- Suffixes

Dictionary
- Guide Words
- Pronunciation
- Spelling
- Word Meaning
- Parts of Speech
- Word History

Glossary
- Terminology of the discipline
- Special meaning of familiar words

Reader's Tip
Using an Electronic Thesaurus

Your word-processing program probably has a thesaurus. In *Word Perfect*, for example, the thesaurus is found in the *Tools* pull-down menu, as one of the *Language* options. To use this, select the word for which you want alternatives by dragging the cursor over the word to highlight it and then clicking on the thesaurus. An array of words will appear, usually both in the *Meanings* box and in the *Replace with Synonyms* box, as you'll find using, for example, the word *right*. Click and highlight a different word other than the one first highlighted in the *Meanings* box; you will get a different array of synonyms. For example, click on the word *sane* and your synonym options will be *normal, rational, sound, reasonable,* and *wise*. The word *right* has forty-nine synonym alternatives on the computer thesaurus in *Microsoft Word*. By moving the down-arrow situated to the right of the word *claim*, you will uncover the word *Antonyms* and the words *wrong, incorrect, erroneous,* and *lenient* will appear as options. Thus, your computer thesaurus has many more words than appear at first glance. Search and choose an option that fits the context of your sentence.

Reader's Tip
Categories of Relationships for Analogies

Synonyms (Similar in meaning)	*Start* is to *begin* as *end* is to *finish*.
Antonyms (Opposite in meaning)	*Retreat* is to *advance* as *tall* is to *short*.
Function, use or purpose (Identifies what something does. Watch for the object (noun) and then the action (verb).)	*Car* is to *drive* as *towel* is to *absorb*.
Classification (Identifies the larger group association)	*Mosquito* is to *insect* as *gasoline* is to *fuel*.
Characteristics and descriptions (Shows qualities or traits)	*Sour* is to *lemon* as *sweet* is to *sugar*.
Degree (Shows variations of intensity)	*Walking* is to *running* as *cool* is to *frozen*.
Part to whole (Shows the larger group)	*Pupil* is to *school* as *sailor* is to *navy*.
Cause and effect (Shows the reason or cause and the result or effect)	*Work* is to *success* as *virus* is to *illness*.

Reader's Tip
Easily Confused Words

capital: city

capitol: building

hole: a depression in the ground

whole: entire

to: in the direction of

too: also

stationary: in a fixed position

stationery: paper

their: belonging to them

there: opposite of here

they're: they are

its: belonging to it

it's: it is

accept: receive

except: all but

your: belonging to you

you're: you are

cite: quote

sight: vision

site: place

threw: launched

through: in one side and out the other

MULTIPLE MEANING MIX

Unravel the confusion. Pronounce and define the words with multiple meanings.

1. The bandage was wound around the wound.

2. The farm was used to produce produce.

3. The dump was so full that it had to refuse more refuse.

4. We must polish the Polish furniture.

5. He could lead if he would get the lead out.

6. The soldier decided to desert his dessert in the desert.

7. Since there is no time like the present, he thought it was time to present the present.

8. A bass was painted on the head of the bass drum.

9. When shot at, the dove dove into the bushes.

10. I did not object to the object.

11. The insurance was invalid for the invalid.

12. There was a row among the oarsmen about how to row.

13. They were too close to the door to close it.

14. The buck does funny things when the does are present.

15. A seamstress and a sewer fell down into a sewer line.

CHAPTER 3 VOCABULARY LESSON QUIZ

Answer the following with correct (C) or incorrect (I).

C _____ 1. A wise employee does not *contradict* her supervisor in front of other workers.

I _____ 2. Tropical plants are common in the *Antarctic*.

C _____ 3. The designer's modern design ideas were the *antithesis* of the client's traditional taste.

I _____ 4. The *prolific* writer has not written a novel since his first and original best-seller.

C _____ 5. The *antagonistic* relationship between the two star quarterbacks was visible as they argued with each other throughout the press conference.

I _____ 6. He was able to *procure* the confidential transcripts, but was unable to obtain them.

I _____ 7. A student who earns an A usually has feelings of *antipathy* towards the coursework.

C _____ 8. The rural hospital did not have an *antidote* for the spider bite, so the patient was flown to a better equipped urban facility.

I _____ 9. *Antacid* is generally used to treat burn victims.

C _____ 10. The *pro-choice* advocates were a minority in the conservative town where their beliefs were often challenged.

Choose the best word from the list to complete the sentence.

proficient	antifreeze	anticlimax	antibodies	contradicted
proliferated	contraband	contrarian	proponents	professed

_____ 11. The border patrol confiscated the smuggled _____ goods.

_____ 12. The sick child's body could not produce enough _____ to fight the disease.

_____ 13. The film began with excitement, but the ending was so dull and predictable that it was an _____ .

_____ 14. The defendant's attorney began the interview as a _____, and presented opposing views to every issue raised.

_____ 15. Enthusiastic _____ of the new highway ignored the fact that it would run right through the historic neighborhood.

_____ 16. Before giving her the engagement ring, he _____ his everlasting love for her.

_____ 17. The _____ keyboard expert accurately typed 80 words per minute.

_____ 18. The wild flowers _____ throughout the fertile field and formed a ribbon of color.

_____ 19. The leaking greenish-yellow _____ formed a puddle beneath the car's radiator.

_____ 20. Her support for a tax increase was _____ by opponents who felt the government should better use existing funds and not get more to waste.

---

11. contraband 12. antibodies 13. anticlimax 14. contrarian 15. proponents
16. professed 17. proficient 18. proliferated 19. antifreeze 20. contradicted

Main Idea

If students can state the main idea and distinguish the significant supporting details, they have the major skills needed for successful college textbook reading. Answering the question, "What point is the author trying to get across?" includes all other skills, even inferential comprehension.

Chapter Objectives:
- What is a main idea?
- What is a topic?
- How do you recognize the difference between general and specific ideas?
- What is a stated main idea?
- What is an unstated main idea?

Transparency Masters:
4.1   Questioning for the Main Idea
4.2   Reader's Tips: *Reading and Studying Psychology* and *Reading and Studying a Short Story*
4.3   Reader's Tips: *Reading and Studying History* and *Selecting a Book*

Suggested Teaching Activities:
1.   For each selection in this book, always ask, "What point is the author trying to get across?" Ask this question so often and about so many different things that it becomes second nature to your students to expect it.
2.   Explain to students that the main idea must be stated in a sentence; anything else is a topic. For example, "Sex" is a topic. "Sex in college" is also a topic. But "Sex in college is good" or "Sex in college is bad" are statements of the author's main idea. The statements are vastly different from the topic. Again, "Sex in college" is not a point.
3.   Often it is very difficult to get students to state the main idea in a sentence. They can state the *topic* fairly easily. In textbooks, the topic is frequently in the title of the chapter or in the

boldface print. View identification of the topic as an application of Piaget's concrete stage of thinking. In asking a student to state the author's main idea, we are requiring a more abstract level of thinking. We are moving the student into Piaget's formal stage of operations. Research indicates that 50 percent of the freshman population comes to college in the concrete stage of thinking. It is no wonder that we have trouble getting our students to state an author's main idea and support it with a few significant details.

4.   Compare the main idea to a thesis statement for an English class theme. This connects writing and reading for students, particularly when the stated main idea is at the beginning or end of a passage.

Incorporating MRL: Put students in groups of two or three and have them work through one of the MRL modules identifying topics and writing main idea sentences.

Reading Workshop Tip: After completing the Main Idea chapter and all of the practice that goes along with it, suggest to students that they journal or blog about their main idea skills. Pose questions such as: Do you feel that your ability to identify the main idea of a passage has improved and in what ways? What advice regarding main idea would you pass along to a classmate who is struggling?

Questioning for the Main Idea

1. **Establish the Topic**

   Who or what is this about?

2. **Identify Key Supporting Terms**

   What are the important details?

3. **Focus on the Message**

   What main idea is the author is trying to convey about the topic?

Reader's Tip
Reading and Studying Psychology

Practice the following exercises as you read a psychology text:

- Seek to understand abstract terms and confusing concepts through the concrete examples that illustrate them.
- Relate psychological theories to yourself and visualize people you know as examples.
- Memorize key terms with definitions and an example, especially for multiple-choice tests.
- Test yourself by turning each bold face heading into a question and recite your answer.
- Since much of psychology is about theories, connect the names of researchers with their theories. Learn characteristics and examples for each theory.
- Compare and contrast theories. For example, how do the social learning theorists differ from the behaviorists?
- Reduce your notes to visual diagrams. For example, to study personality theories, draw charts to list the comparative elements.

Reader's Tip
Reading and Studying a Short Story

Ask yourself the following questions as you read a short story:
- How would you describe the main character? What other characters are well-developed? What is the purpose of the "flat" characters? What do the characters learn? How do the characters change?
- What is the main conflict in the story? What are the steps in the development of the plot? What is the climax? What is the resolution?
- What is the theme of the story? What universal truth did you learn from the story?
- When and where is the story set? How does the setting affect the theme?
- Who is telling the story? How does this point of view affect the message?
- What is the tone of the author? What mood is the author trying to create?
- What symbols provide vivid images that enrich the theme?
- What is your evaluation of the author's work?

Reader's Tip
Reading and Studying History

- Know the *who*, *what*, *when*, *where*, and *why* for significant people, places, documents, and events.
- Seek to understand the cause-and-effect relationships between events and their causes, results, and consequences.
- Use timelines to familiarize yourself with chronologies to get an overall picture of parallel or overlapping events.
- Learn significant dates to provide a framework for grouping and understanding events.
- Look at maps of the region being studied.
- Distinguish between fact and opinion, and compare your conclusions with the historian's interpretation.

Reader's Tip
Selecting a Book

After locating a book that looks interesting, investigate further using these strategies.

- Read the book jacket. Do the quotes from reviewers seem valid or clipped out of context? Do the blurbs introducing the book entice you? Has the author written other books that you have enjoyed? If the book is nonfiction, what are the author's credentials?
- Read the first page and at least one other page. Do you like the writing style? Is it comfortable for you to read? Does the first page grab your attention?
- If nonfiction, look at the illustrations and read the captions. Are you intrigued?
- If nonfiction, review the table of contents and scan the index. Is this material that you want to learn more about?

Selection 1: Sleeping and Dreaming

Answer with T (true) or F (false).

Comprehension Quiz (for prereading or postreading)

T _____ 1. During REM sleep the brain waves are similar to those of a waking period.

T _____ 2. Everyone dreams.

T _____ 3. Some theorists suggest that dreaming is good for your mental health.

T _____ 4. Dreams are sometimes symbolic of daily life.

F _____ 5. REM sleep occurs in over 80 percent of the total sleeping time.

Vocabulary Quiz (for prereading or postreading)

F _____ 1. A person who is *unconscious* is not able to breathe.

T _____ 2. The statement, "He is, but he isn't" is a *paradox*.

T _____ 3. A new gas station should be *convenient* to customers.

T _____ 4. White is sometimes used to *symbolize* purity.

T _____ 5. A boy who bullies others is not usually popular with his classmates.

F _____ 6. *Idling* away your time is a good way to achieve success.

F _____ 7. *Depriving* a person of an education will usually help him or her get a better job.

T _____ 8. The authorship of a story is *ascribed* to the writer.

F _____ 9. A *critical* question is of little importance.

T _____ 10. *Synchronized* watches tell the same time.

Selection 2: Shatter Proof

Answer with T (true) or F (false).

Comprehension Quiz (for prereading or postreading)

T _____ 1. The assassin wanted to watch Mr. Williams prepare his drink because he was worried that Mr. Williams might poison him.

F _____ 2. In the assassin's view, he chose not to take the $30,000 painting because it would remind him of the distasteful act of murdering Mr. Williams.

T _____ 3. Mr. Williams compared his boredom with the jade figurine to the boredom of his life with his wife.

F _____ 4. The glass that Mr. Williams took to the detective agency was the one from the wall safe.

T _____ 5. Mr. Williams tricked the assassin by bluffing about whose glass was in the wall safe.

F _____ 6. The author implies that Mr. Smith will eventually kill Mr. Williams.

F _____ 7. Mr. Williams diverts the assassin's attention by revealing a secret door hidden within the bookshelves.

T _____ 8. The author implies that the assassin is forced to shoot Mrs. Williams for his own protection.

F _____ 9. It was stated in the passage that Mr. Williams did not go to the police because he, himself, was a criminal.

T _____ 10. Mr. Williams expected that his wife would divorce him.

Vocabulary Quiz (for prereading or postreading)

F _____ 1. A *decanter* is a vase designed for flowers.

F _____ 2. *Morbid* thoughts are of joy rather than sorrow.

T _____ 3. A successful psychologist benefits from a keen *insight* into human behavior.

F _____ 4. A *davenport* is a chair that converts into a comfortable recliner.

F _____ 5. *Authentic* designer purses are usually sold on the street by illegal vendors.

T _____ 6. A real estate agent earns a *commission* that is typically based on a percentage of the sales price for a home.

F _____ 7. An *incorruptible* public official can be paid by businesses for vote changes and favors.

T _____ 8. In the face of danger, *fortitude* is needed.

F _____ 9. *Pertinent* information is secondary rather than primary.

T _____ 10. To *commiserate* with a friend is to extend your sympathy and kindness.

SELECTION 3: THE DREAM OF NONVIOLENT REFORM

Answer with T *(true) or* F *(false).*

Comprehension Quiz (for prereading or postreading)

F   ____ 1. King's famous "I Have a Dream" speech was made at the Washington Monument.

T   ____ 2. The gathering in Washington at which King made his famous speech was to celebrate the centennial of the Emancipation Proclamation.

F   ____ 3. The speakers who presented before King at the Washington gathering had electrified the crowd.

T   ____ 4. The words "Free at last!" are quoted from an old black spiritual.

T   ____ 5. King went to Memphis for a garbage workers strike.

F   ____ 6. Black Power militants requested that King come to Memphis.

T   ____ 7. The demonstrations in Memphis had become violent before King's arrival.

F   ____ 8. King was shot on the balcony of the Masonic Temple while making a speech in Memphis.

T   ____ 9. Before his death in prison, James Earl Ray denied having shot King.

T   ____ 10. The FBI harassed King in an attempt to indicate that he was under the influence of Communism.

Vocabulary Quiz (for prereading or postreading)

F   ____ 1. *Sweltering* weather is cooler than usual.

F   ____ 2. A *centennial* celebration marks 50 years of existence.

F   ____ 3. *Oppressive* heat is easily tolerated.

F   ____ 4. A *podium* is a chair that is positioned in the front row on a stage.

T   ____ 5. A *resonant* voice is strong and forceful.

F   ____ 6. A *galvanized* crowd is restless and unfocused.

T   ____ 7. If justice prevails, *spurious* evidence should not lead to a conviction.

T   ____ 8. *Dire* poverty is desperate and excessive.

T   ____ 9. If romantic love is *recanted*, a breakup may likely follow.

T   ____ 10. If you are *compelled* to dance, you feel the need to rise and move to the beat.

CHAPTER 4 VOCABULARY LESSON QUIZ

Choose an appropriate word from the list to complete each of the following sentences.

antecedent	postscript	postponed	preamble	precocious
posthumously	premonition	posterity	prelude	antebellum

_____ 1. The tennis match was briefly _____ due to rain.

_____ 2. The child believed that her nightmare was a _____
that her father was in danger.

_____ 3. In Charleston, South Carolina, stately _____ homes
are open for tours.

_____ 4. A CD with the deceased artist's most popular songs was
released _____ as a final tribute.

_____ 5. The _____ added to the letter must have been
written hastily, because it is barely legible.

_____ 6. Although the _____ was rather melancholy, the
presentation of the entire musical composition was uplifting.

_____ 7. The grandmother organized the old photos into albums for
_____.

_____ 8. The curious toddler asked intelligent questions and appeared to
be quite _____.

_____ 9. The paper was filled with errors, including _____ and
pronoun disagreements such as using *it* for *workers*.

_____ 10. Although she felt nervous, she precisely recited the famous
_____ to the Constitution in front of her entire class.

1. delayed 2. premonition 3. antebellum 4. posthumously 5. postscript
6. prelude 7. posterity 8. precocious 9. antecedents 10. preamble

Answer with T *(true) or* F *(false).*

F _____ 11. A *predecessor* is the most recently hired staff member.

T _____ 12. By saying, "Your reputation *precedes* you," others indicate knowing about your reputation before meeting you.

F _____ 13. *Antescripts* are usually found in the back of books.

F _____ 14. The *postnatal* phase occurs during the last month of pregnancy.

T _____ 15. Trials can be moved to a new location if the judge believes that local jurors are *prejudiced*.

T _____ 16. *Antennae* allow insects to sense their surroundings.

T _____ 17. Many Harvard alumni regard Harvard as the *preeminent* university in the United States.

T _____ 18. The joyous New Year's Eve celebration *antecedes* the traditional Rose Bowl Parade on New Year's day.

F _____ 19. The artifact appeared to be relatively new, thus the archaeologists classified it as *antediluvian*.

F _____ 20. He summarized his speech with a powerful *preamble*.

Supporting Details and Organizational Patterns

The most common organizational format in college textbooks (except in history and literature texts) is to introduce and define a term or concept, and then give examples or elaborate. If students learn to recognize this pattern, they will be less intimidated by college textbook reading.

Chapter Objectives:
- What is a detail?
- How do you recognize levels of importance?
- What is a major detail?
- What is a minor detail?
- What organizational patterns are used in textbooks?
- How do transitional words signal organization?

Transparency Masters:
5.1   Reader's Tips: *Distinguishing Major and Minor Details* and *Following Directions*
5.2   Patterns of Organizations
5.3   Reader's Tip: *Patterns of Organization and Signal Words*
5.4   Reader's Tip: *Choosing a Magazine*
Casebook: Reader's Tips: *Reading and Studying Letters of Opinion* and *Reading and Studying a News or Feature Article*
5.5   Think Critically about Beauty

Casebook: "What is beauty?" Teaching Suggestion

Suggested Teaching Activities:
1.   To introduce this chapter, bring some psychology, sociology, or business books to class and show students how page after page follows a similar organizational pattern. Show them how

most of the words in the biology book are defined in the text itself. As an assignment, ask students to bring in examples from textbooks in other courses and identify the predominant patterns of organization.

2.   This chapter also reinforces the concept of *main idea*. Encourage students to mark this textbook so that they are more aware graphically of how the different parts make up the whole. Ask them to tear out the pages so that you can check and see that adequate, but not excessive, markings have been made. This is also a beginning stage of note taking. Students can see how recognizing the organizational pattern can help them mark the text for later study.

3.   To reinforce the first section on levels of importance, ask students to visit an Internet art shop and find two paintings that they would like to purchase if money were no object. The following Web site is well organized and should produce interesting results: Paintingsdirect.com.

Ask students to print the chosen paintings and to use at least three levels of classification to find each painting. The levels include the following: artist, style, country of origin, color, size, and price. They can be used in any level of importance according to the desires of the purchaser.

4.   Cut up paragraphs into sentence strips and have students working in groups organize the sentences into logical order. Students enjoy an activity of this type and it reinforces the idea of structure or organization in writing.

Incorporating MRL: Guide students to the Pearson Study Skills website in MRL and review the resources under Taking Notes on Readings. Along with study tips that illustrate uses of various patterns of organization, the web resources tab links to several web sites that provide additional information on graphic organizers.

Reading Workshop Tip: Encourage students to think about the organization of the novel they are currently reading and write about it in their journals. They may notice that their novel's plot unfolds through flashbacks or through characters' points of views. Pose questions regarding why the author chose the organization/development of the plot. Is it effective? Confusing? How might it be better? Etc.

Reader's Tip
Distinguishing Major and Minor Details

To determine which details give major or minor support, first identify the author's main point and then ask yourself the following questions:

1. What details are needed to explain or prove the main idea? (These are major details that give primary support.)
2. What details are included just to make the passage more interesting? (These are minor details that provide a secondary level of support.)

Reader's Tip
Following Directions

- Change your mindset from normal reading and commit to a different kind of task.
- Read to get an overview so that you have a general idea of the task and can make a plan.
- Assemble the necessary equipment, estimate the time, and find a helper if needed.
- Read each step sequentially, and do as directed. Move from word to word and phrase to phrase for a clear understanding. Read aloud if necessary.
- Use numbers, letters, and guide words such as *first, next, before, after, then,* and *now* to maintain sequence. Insert your own numbers if steps are not sequenced.
- Visualize the process. Consult the diagram. Draw your own diagram if none exists.
- Think logically and keep your goal in mind.

Patterns of Organization

- **Simple Listing**

- **Classification**

- **Definitions with Examples**

- **Description**

- **Time Order, Sequence, or Narration**

- **Comparison and Contrast**

- **Cause and Effect**

Reader's Tip

Patterns of Organization and Signal Words

Addition:
(providing additional information)

furthermore, again, also, further, moreover, besides, likewise

Cause and Effect:
(showing one element as producing or causing a result or effect)

because, for this reason, consequently, hence, as a result, thus, due to, therefore

Classification:
(dividing items into groups or categories)

groups, categories, elements, classes, parts

Comparison:
(listing similarities among items)

in a similar way, similar, parallels, likewise, in a like manner

Contrast:
(listing differences among items)

on the other hand, bigger than, but, however, conversely, on the contrary, although, nevertheless

Definition:
(initially defining a concept and expanding with examples and restatements)

can be defined, means, for example, like

Description:
(listing characteristics or details)

is, as, like, could be described

Generalization and Example:
(explaining with examples to illustrate)

to restate, that is, for example, to illustrate, for instance

Location or Spatial Order:
(identifying the whereabouts of objects)

next to, near, below, above, close by, within, without, adjacent to, beside, around, to the right or left side, opposite

Simple Listing:
(randomly listing items in a series)

also, another, several, for example

Summary:
(condensing major points)

in conclusion, briefly, to sum up, in short, in a nutshell

Time Order, Sequence, or Narration:
(listing events in order of occurrence)

first, second, finally, after, before, next, later, now, at last, until, thereupon, while, during

Reader's Tip

Choosing a Magazine

- Read the lead article headlines and the table of contents to find articles of interest to you.

- Flip through the magazine and read article titles and boxed article excerpts.

- Read several *Letters to the Editor*.

- Decide, purchase, and enjoy!

Reader's Tip

Reading and Studying Letters of Opinion

Ask yourself the following questions as you read editorials or letters of opinion:

- What event prompted the letter?

- What is the thesis or opinion being promoted by the author?

- Do the details prove the opinion?

- What is left out?

- Are the sources, facts, and other support credible?

Reader's Tip

Reading and Studying a News or Feature Article

- Preview the headline and photographs.
- Find the facts: *who, what, when, were, why,* and *how.*
- Consider how the angle or focus of a feature story differs from a straight news story.
- Evaluate the credibility of the sources cited.
- When reading a feature story, observe the number of facts compared with the number of opinions.
- Look for bias or judgment on the part of the reporter.

SELECTION 1: BECOMING HEALTHY

Answer with T *(true) or* F *(false).*

Comprehension Quiz (for prereading or postreading)

F   ____   1. You can be healthy simply by deciding to be healthy.

T   ____   2. Self-doubt comes from a feeling that other people will not find you acceptable.

T   ____   3. Expressing your feelings to other people can reduce tension.

T   ____   4. Being loved is a health-producing experience.

T   ____   5. Other people help us define who we are.

F   ____   6. Happiness follows from what you *say*, not what you *do*.

T   ____   7. The persistent feeling of dread can result in physical ailments.

T   ____   8. To overcome depression, the author suggests that a person should become active, get to work, and begin to be involved.

F   ____   9. The author believes that self-understanding can be achieved in isolation with your own deep thoughts and feelings.

T   ____   10. The author believes that living fully means being involved in something outside yourself.

Vocabulary Quiz (for prereading or postreading)

F   ____   1. A *pervasive* odor is easy to eliminate.

F   ____   2. Hikers usually want to *encounter* a bear while in the forest.

T   ____   3. *Excessive* drinking can lead to alcoholism.

F   ____   4. *Timidity* is a desirable quality in a public speaker.

F   ____   5. Human *frailty* is a sign of strength.

T   ____   6. A *chronic* illness seems to be with you all the time.

T   ____   7. A new *perspective* can be a different point of view.

F   ____   8. *Profound* sorrow is insincere regret.

T   ____   9. Sometimes *competency* is measured by a standardized test.

F   ____   10. To look at yourself in the mirror is an example of *self-transcendence*.

SELECTION 2: CONFIDENCE GAMES MAY BE A SHELL GAME SCENE

Answer with T *(true) or* F *(false).*

Comprehension Quiz (for prereading or postreading)

T _____ 1. According to the author, confidence artists prey on the frailties of human nature.

T _____ 2. According to the passage, many victims do not report confidence scams.

T _____ 3. In the pigeon drop, the victims must pay to share money that is found in a wallet or envelope.

F _____ 4. In the bank examiner scheme, the con artist goes with the victim inside the bank to withdraw money.

F _____ 5. In the inheritance scam, the victim receives the money but it is quickly taken away.

T _____ 6. In the three-card monte scam, the victim wins initially.

F _____ 7. In the C.O.D. scam, the person to whom the package is addressed is the one who pays the money.

F _____ 8. In the money-making-machine scam, American money is used to make German money.

T _____ 9. In the Nigerian oil con, the con artists place advertisements in newspapers to find victims.

F _____ 10. In the Nigerian oil con, the price of oil quoted to the victim is less than half of the current market price.

Vocabulary Quiz (for prereading or postreading)

T _____ 1. The phrase "annals of time" *suggests* the records of the past.

F _____ 2. Cunning crooks lack *guile*.

T _____ 3. A *monetary* reward is a cash payment.

F _____ 4. A *swindle* is a deal that is lawful and just.

F _____ 5. A *sleight* of hand is obvious to most onlookers.

T _____ 6. *Fraudulent* documents are created illegally.

T _____ 7. A *phony* driver's license is a fake identification.

T _____ 8. *Affluent* customers have spendable income.

F _____ 9. *Perishable* goods do not quickly spoil.

51

Selection 3: A Short History of Medicine

Answer with T *(true) or* F *(false).*

Comprehension Quiz (for prereading or postreading)

F   _____ 1. Cancer is a modern disease.

T   _____ 2. The oldest description of cancer dates back to approximately 1600 B. C.

T   _____ 3. Hippocrates believed a balance of body fluids meant a person was cancer free.

F   _____ 4. Scientists were able to prove the trauma theory through animal research.

T   _____ 5. Several viruses such as HIV and HPVs are linked to cancer.

T   _____ 6. James Watson and Francis Crick received the Nobel prize for their work in DNA.

T   _____ 7. Scientists now know that cancer is caused by a change in DNA structure.

F   _____ 8. The recent discovery of BRCA1 and BRCA2 has led to a cure for breast cancer.

T   _____ 9. Familial cancer occurs less often than spontaneous cancer.

F   _____ 10. Cancer research prior to the 20th century has no influence on current research.

Vocabulary Quiz (for prereading or postreading)

T   _____ 1. A physician in *oncology* specializes in tumors.

T   _____ 2. A *pathologist* is an expert in diseases.

F   _____ 3. Someone diagnosed with *osteosarcoma* will probably lose his vision.

T   _____ 4. A *carcinoma* should be examined by a physician as soon as possible.

T   _____ 5. *Autopsies* are performed to determine cause of death.

F   _____ 6. *Lymph* cancer suggests bone cancer.

T   _____ 7. Joe's persistent cough was a *chronic* irritation to his classmates.

F   _____ 8. Herman Hospital's *Trauma* Center specializes in psychiatric treatment.

T   _____ 9. Second hand smoke contains harmful *carcinogens*.

T   _____ 10. A *mutation* in genes can lead to a cancer diagnosis.

CHAPTER 5 VOCABULARY LESSON QUIZ

Answer with T *(true) or* F *(false).*

T   ____ 1. *Bimonthly* meetings take place every other month.

T   ____ 2. The children of many recent Hispanic immigrants are *bilingual*, which means they speak Spanish and English.

T   ____ 3. A *monochromatic* flower arrangement may have a variety of flowers, but they are all the same color.

T   ____ 4. Since a city such as San Diego is home to people of many different races and ethnicities, it might be called a *polyethnic* city.

F   ____ 5. A woman who practices *polyandry* has pledged never to be married.

F   ____ 6. *Polygons* are shapes with many curves and no angles.

T   ____ 7. *Bifocals* are helpful to those who have trouble seeing both close up and far away.

T   ____ 8. Having the same meal for breakfast everyday can be *monotonous* to some.

T   ____ 9. Plaid fabrics with beautiful colors offer several options for matching colors since they are *polychromatic*.

F   ____ 10. *Bigamy* is the practice of filing for divorce without being legally married.

Choose the best word from the list to fit the following descriptions.

| polymorphic | biweekly | monogamy | polydactyl | monocle |
| bipartisan | polyglot | monarchy | polygamy | monotone |

_____ 11. multilingual

_____ 12. eyeglass

_____ 13. rule of king or queen

_____ 14. balanced politically

_____ 15. traditional American marriage

_____ 16. unchanging voice

_____ 17. every two weeks

_____ 18. more than 10 fingers

_____ 19. many spouses

_____ 20. many forms

11. polyglot 12. monocle 13. monarchy 14. bipartisan 15. monogamy
16. monotone 17. biweekly 18. polydactyl 19. polygamy 20. polymorphic

CASE BOOK 1: WHAT IS BEAUTY? SUGGESTED TEACHING ACTIVITY

The case books are designed as a reading-across-the-curriculum experience to give students an opportunity to research, synthesize, and reflect on a single topic after reading about it in three different disciplines. As students become more educated on the topic, viewing it from different perspectives, their original opinions tend to broaden and change. The result becomes real-life problem solving.

Begin the case book adventure by documenting present beliefs. Ask students to fill out the inventory on what beauty means to them. Discuss their responses and encourage them to be open-minded about new ideas while reading the four selections on beauty.

Use the comprehension questions at the end of each selection to encourage personal growth. Students may be battling their own biases and preconceived notions. Expect deeper thinking and some soul-searching. Finish the chapter with the concluding inventory and compare the results.

Use the quotations on the following page to introduce the topic.

THINK CRITICALLY ABOUT BEAUTY

Which of the quotes below reflects your views on physical beauty? On a separate sheet of paper, explain why you picked this quote to describe your views on beauty.

"Beauty is not in the face; beauty is a light in the heart."

-- Kahlil Gibran

"Beauty is how you feel inside, and it reflects in your eyes. It is not something physical."

-- Sophia Loren

"Beauty comes in all sizes—not just size 5."

-- Roseanne

"Always remember that true beauty comes from within—from within bottles, jars, compacts, and tubes."

-- Peter's Almanac

"It's beauty that captures your attention; personality which captures your heart."

-- Anonymous

"I'm in the public eye, so I don't care who knows what I get done. If I see something sagging, dragging, or bagging, I get it sucked, tucked, or plucked."

-- Dolly Parton

Chapter Six

Textbook Learning

Reading for recreation and reading to learn involve two different purposes. Explain the differences and then begin a discussion of study strategies. Ask students how many times they have heard classmates say, "I really studied for my midterm exam; I read all the material three times." Talk about what happens during rereading and why it is not an effective study method. Point out the need in study reading to organize information to facilitate future learning.

Chapter Objectives:
- What is annotating?
- What is the Cornell method of notetaking?
- How do you write a summary?
- How can you use outlining?
- What is mapping?

Transparency Masters:

6.1   Organizing Textbooks for Learning
6.2   Reader's Tips: *How to Write a Summary* and *Creating an Outline*
6.3   Reader's Tips: *Reading in Communications* and *Defining Your Topic*
6.4   Sample Outline: *Six Types of Love*
6.5   Sample Outline: Selection 1 *Behavior Change*
6.6   Sample Outline: Selection 2 *Goya Foods*
6.7   Sample Outline: Selection 3 *Eye Communication*

Suggested Teaching Activities:

1.   Getting students to understand the importance of taking notes with the intent to learn from those notes is difficult to do. Often they are so intent on copying, they forget to think about what they are writing. Start this activity by having students draw both sides of a dollar bill (or a penny, anything they

see frequently) from memory. Look at two or three student drawings together on the document camera. Next, as a class, thoroughly examine both sides of a dollar bill, pointing out details in the symbols and their meanings. (A quick online search will turn up the symbols and meanings for you.) Last, have students draw the dollar bill again. They should be quite impressed with the detail they recall on the second drawing. Explain that their notes were better the second time because they examined the dollar bill with the intent to remember the details. After a week or two, see how well students can recall the details by having them draw the bill again.

2.   Cut a longer selection into sentence strips and place them in an envelope. Have students working in groups of three or four arrange the sentences into an outline which they can then type into a Word document. Compare outlines on the document camera.

3.   Students can take the same sentences in activity two and condense them into key phrases and place them on a concept map.

Incorporating MRL: Encourage students to visit the Pearson Study Skills website in MRL and review the resources under *Reading Textbooks* and *Taking Notes on Readings*. Along with study tips that illustrate uses of various patterns of organization, the web resources tab links to several web sites that provide additional information on organizing notes into graphic organizers.

Reading Workshop Tip: To further the notion of encouraging childhood reading as discussed in the chapter, urge your students to read to a child. Perhaps this can be something they do with a child of their own, or a younger sibling or cousin. If your campus has a child development center, students would benefit from visiting the center and witnessing a reading circle, or better yet, reading to the children themselves. They can then write about the experience in their journal.

ORGANIZING TEXTBOOKS FOR LEARNING

- Annotating

- Notetaking

- Summarizing

- Outlining

- Mapping

Reader's Tip
How to Write a Summary

1. Remember your purpose; be brief.
2. Underline the key ideas in the text you want to include.
3. Begin your summary with a general statement, the main idea that unites the key ideas.
4. Include the key ideas that support the general statement. Link these ideas in sentences, and show their significance.
5. Delete irrelevant or trivial information.
6. Delete redundant information.
7. Use your own words to show your understanding of the material. Don't try to camouflage a lack of comprehension.
8. Do not include your opinions or anything that is not in the original.

Reader's Tip
Creating an Outline

The following is the format for a model outline. Notice how the numbers, letters, and indentations show the importance of an idea.

Main Point or Topic
I. Primary supporting idea #1
   A. Secondary supporting detail
   B. Secondary supporting detail
   C. Secondary supporting detail
II. Primary supporting idea #2
   A. Secondary supporting detail
   B. Secondary supporting detail
     1. Minor supporting detail or example
     2. Minor supporting detail or example
III. Primary supporting idea #3
   A. Secondary supporting detail
   B. Secondary supporting detail

Reader's Tip

Reading and Studying in Communications

Ask yourself the following questions as you read a communications text:

- How can I improve as a communicator and a conversationalist?
- How do I react to other people? Am I open to ideas?
- How can I become a more valuable group member or a more productive group leader?
- Am I afraid to speak in public? How can I lessen that fear?
- What actions and expressions should be avoided in opening and closing a speech?

Reader's Tip

Defining Your Topic

To define your research topic, consider:

Geography: Pick a specific area.

Time Frame: Limit the time period under examination.

Interest Groups: Narrow your research by appropriate descriptors such as age, gender, or occupation.

Academic Discipline: What college or department would study this subject?

SIX TYPES OF LOVE (SAMPLE OUTLINE)

I. Eros: Beauty and Sensuality
   A. Focus: physical attractiveness
   B. Idealized and unattainable image of beauty
   C. Often unfulfilled
   D. Report highest levels of satisfied lovers

II. Ludus: Entertainment and Excitement
   A. Focus: a game to be played for fun
   B. Emotions and passion held in control
   C. Self-controlled and manipulative
   D. Report dissatisfaction with less happiness, friendship, and trust

III. Storge: Peaceful and Slow
   A. Focus: companion relationship with shared interests
   B. Lacks passion and intensity
   C. Develops over time and sex is late
   D. Mutual caring and respect

IV. Pragma: Practical and Traditional
   A. Focus: meet needs for a good life
   B. Concern over social qualifications
   C. Family, background, and job important
   D. Relies on logic rather than feelings

V. Manic: Elation and Depression
   A. Focus: has to possess the beloved completely
   B. Loves, worries, and fears intensely
   C. Obsessive and driven
   D. Wishes to be possessed

VI. Agape: Compassionate and Selfless
   A. Focus: self-giving love
   B. Love for strangers
   C. Spiritual love offered without gain
   D. Related to female life satisfaction

SELECTION 1: BEHAVIOR CHANGE

Answer with T *(true) or* F *(false).*

Comprehension Quiz (for prereading or postreading)

F _____ 1. Behavior changes are most likely to succeed if they start at the Action Stage; that is, if they start with the change itself.

T _____ 2. In the Contemplation Stage, the person begins to think about the need to change.

T _____ 3. The Maintenance Stage requires vigilance, attention to detail, and long-term commitment.

F _____ 4. During the Termination Stage, the person has given up trying to change.

F _____ 5. A "positive reinforcement" is a reward that is given to decrease the likelihood that a behavior change will occur.

F _____ 6. The final of the five stages of change is action.

T _____ 7. The process of taking small individual steps to change one piece of the larger behavior is called shaping.

T _____ 8. The technique of doing an imaginary mental and verbal rehearsal of a challenging behavioral situation is visualization.

F _____ 9. A situational inducement refers to observing and imitating the behavior of others.

F _____ 10. Changing negative self-talk to positive self-talk is called blocking.

Vocabulary Quiz (for prereading or postreading)

T _____ 1. To *coax* a friend is to persuade toward action.

T _____ 2. An *acknowledgement* for a gift can be a written note of appreciation.

F _____ 3. If you *languish* on the weekend, your days are filled with accomplishment.

T _____ 4. Adult *vigilance* is required to keep toddlers safe.

F _____ 5. A *commitment* to a project means that you are not fully supportive.

T _____ 6. A *scenario* resembles a glimpse of a play.

T _____ 7. An *inducement* to study might be a monetary reward for A's.

T _____ 8. A *premise* is a supposition that may or may not be true.

F _____ 9. *Irrational* thought follows a logical sequence.

T _____ 10. To *resort* to punishment means that in desperation you choose that option.

BEHAVIOR CHANGE
(SAMPLE OUTLINE)

I. Stages of Change

    A. Precontemplation – no current intention of changing

    B. Contemplation – recognizes problem and need for change

    C. Preparation – arrived at a plan for action

    D. Action – begins to follow the action plan

    E. Maintenance – vigilance of long-term commitment

    F. Termination – behavior ingrained as part of life

II. Choosing a Behavior: Change Strategy

    A. Shaping – take individual steps to change smaller parts of behavior

    B. Visualization – imagined rehearsal to visualize planned action

    C. Modeling – observation of others to learn

    D. Controlling the situation – situational inducement

    E. Reinforcement – positive reward

    F. Changing Self-Talk – change the way you think and talk to yourself

        1. Rational Emotive therapy: change irrational self-talk

        2. Meichenbaum self-instruction methods: deep breathing and coping instructions

        3. Blocking/Thought stopping: Block negative thoughts and force alternative thoughts

SELECTION 2: GOYA FOODS

Answer with T *(true) or* F *(false).*

Comprehension Quiz (for prereading or postreading)

T   ____ 1. Goya Foods requests the "shop within a shop" setup for its product displays.

F   ____ 2. Goya Foods caters mostly to immigrants from Spain rather than South America.

F   ____ 3. Goya Foods regularly pays a "slotting fee" to businesses.

F   ____ 4. Goya Foods is a new company and has not been in business long.

F   ____ 5. Crossover sales are defined as people who buy only Latino products.

T   ____ 6. Surveys indicate that the majority of Latinos believe that brands are very important in deciding where to shop.

T   ____ 7. Latinos on the average shop for groceries more than two times per week.

F   ____ 8. The founder of Goya Foods immigrated to New York from Mexico.

T   ____ 9. Goya Foods is the largest family-owned food company in the United States.

F   ____ 10. According to the passage, the menu at the Smithsonian Institute features Goya Foods.

Vocabulary Quiz (for prereading or postreading)

T   ____ 1. When *consumer* spending rises, more people are typically making purchases.

T   ____ 2. Early pioneers are in the *forefront* of a movement for change.

F   ____ 3. A *trend* is a fashion that is classical and long lasting.

T   ____ 4. Basketball is a game that is *dominated* by height and quick reactions.

T   ____ 5. If your company is *positioned* in the soft drink business, you probably compete with Coca Cola.

T   ____ 6. If students *strive* to earn "A's," they work hard for good grades.

T   ____ 7. *Gauging* a demand involves measuring a need.

F   ____ 8. *Demographic* reports study roads and transportation.

T   ____ 9. If you *garner* an award, you are honored with a prize.

F   ____ 10. The *core* group is most likely composed of seldom seen supporters.

GOYA FOODS
(SAMPLE OUTLINE)

I. Goya Foods
    A. Hispanic powerhouse
    B. Organized differently at supermarkets
    C. Shop-within-a-shop

II. Caters to Ethnic Group
    A. Latino population
    B. Based on Latino consumer habits
    C. Imports needed foods

III. Goya Foods Works with Retailers
    A. Pays "slotting fee"
    B. Few crossover sales

IV. Marketing Studies
    A. Loyalty of Latino shoppers
    B. 85% shop at supermarkets
    C. Brand names important
    D. Buying power equals half trillion dollars yearly
    E. Shop 4.7 time a week

V. Background information
    A. 70-year-old company
    B. Began in Manhattan as small business
    C. Has become largest family-owned food company
        in U.S.
    D. Always been involved with community endeavors

SELECTION 3: EYE COMMUNICATION

Answer with T *(true) or* F *(false).*

Comprehension Quiz (for prereading or postreading)

T _____ 1. According to the passage, direct eye contact in Japan is viewed as a lack of respect.

T _____ 2. In America, eye contact that falls short of the average amount suggests the other person is uninterested.

F _____ 3. Studies indicate that speakers look at listeners more than listeners look at speakers.

T _____ 4. The passage implies that eye movements can be used to end a conversation.

T _____ 5. According to the passage, photos of women with small pupils were characterized as cold and selfish.

Vocabulary Quiz (for prereading or postreading)

T _____ 1. The *duration* of a journey is the length of time spent in travel.

T _____ 2. To *gaze* at a celebrity is to turn your head toward fame.

T _____ 3. To *perceive* the outcome is to predict the future.

T _____ 4. To *compensate* a worker is to pay for services.

F _____ 5. To *avert* a problem is to ignore the issue.

F _____ 6. An *auditory* disturbance can be seen but not heard.

T _____ 7. An *intuitive* thinker can sometimes sense an appropriate solution.

T _____ 8. *Dilated* pupils allow entry of more light than normal.

T _____ 9. *Constricted* blood vessels hinder the flow of blood.

F _____ 10. A *profound* limitation should not hinder performance.

EYE COMMUNICATION
(SAMPLE OUTLINE)

I. Message Communicated

    A. Duration: cultural limits

    B. Direction: cultural differences and suggested attention

    C. Quality: suggests interest levels

II. Functions of Eye Contact

    A. Monitor feedback

    B. Secure attention and interest of listeners

    C. Regulate or control the conversation

    D. Signal nature of relationship

    E. Signal status and aggression

    F. Compensate for increased physical distance

III. Eye Avoidance

    A. Civil inattention

    B. Lack of interest

IV. Pupil Dilation

    A. Seen as more attractive

    B. Reveals level of emotional arousal

CHAPTER 6 VOCABULARY LESSON QUIZ

Choose the best word from the list to complete each of the following sentences:

audio	envision	audition	evident	vocational
evoked	audible	convocation	audit	visas

_____ 1. The coach asked the football players to use their imaginations and _____ themselves executing each play that he diagramed.

_____ 2. The brownies tasted so bitter it was _____ that he didn't follow the recipe with enough sugar.

_____ 3. The conductor's voice was barely _____ above the noise of the subway.

_____ 4. Once the surround-sound system was installed, the _____ was crystal clear.

_____ 5. After two years in a _____ school, she was a certified electrician.

_____ 6. The whole family is planning to attend his graduation _____.

_____ 7. The snow _____ memories of growing up in the Rocky Mountains of Colorado.

_____ 8. American tourists need passports but not _____ to visit Mexico.

_____ 9. The pianist beamed with confidence that his _____ for the jazz band was outstanding and he would be asked to join.

_____ 10. Dramatic changes in earnings can trigger an IRS _____.

---

1. envision 2. evident 3. audible 4. audio 5. vocational
6. convocation 7. evoked 8. visas 9. audition 10 audit

Answer with T *(true) or* F *(false).*

T   ____ 11. A *visionary* entrepreneur can make money by picturing future business needs.

T   ____ 12. Hotel rooms with *vistas* are sometimes more expensive than rooms without views.

F   ____ 13. Since prayer is no longer allowed, public school children begin each day with an *invocation*.

T   ____ 14. Students seldom *vociferously* oppose homework assignments over holiday breaks.

T   ____ 15. In some companies, employees must keep identification badges *visible* at all times.

T   ____ 16. Hearing aids can help individuals with *auditory* problems.

F   ____ 17. Pro tennis players do not wear *visors* during matches because they are distracting.

T   ____ 18. Passion for your *avocation* can become greater than your job interests.

T   ____ 19. Bill Cosby *evokes* humor into his descriptions of family situations.

T   ___ 20. Instant solutions to car problems are not always *evident* even to skilled mechanics.

Chapter Seven

Test-Taking Strategies

In this chapter I have tried to give test-taking advice and teach test-taking strategies in an interactive manner. The initial advice is common sense, but many students are unaware of the obvious results of these actions. I used the anecdotes to freshen the approach for the students. The purpose is to make them think and later react in a class discussion.

Chapter Objectives:
- Can your physical condition affect your test score?
- Are test questions predictable?
- How can you keep your mind on what you are reading?
- How are standardized test items made especially tricky?
- How do you organize an essay response?

Transparency Masters:
7.1 Taking Standardized Tests
7.2 Major Question Types
7.3 Reader's Tip: *Types of Test Passages*
7.4 Reader's Tip: *Remembering Information*

Suggested Teaching Activities:
1. The comprehension skills are those that are taught throughout the text. This is a chapter that needs the explanations offered in the other chapters to make it complete. To reduce student anxiety, it is especially important to show them that comprehension questions are predictable. After discussing the major question types, bring in some standardized tests and ask students to identify the types. Particularly point out that only vocabulary and a few detail items can be answered without a clear understanding of the passage.

2.   Chapter Seven needs a lot of class discussion and modeling. It is particularly difficult for students to write test items, but remember that the ability to write test items is not the ultimate goal. Use this strategy to give students insight into what is being done to them by the test makers. Create some of the items in class, and then have students write others while working in groups of three.

Most of the answers for the exercises in this chapter will come from the students themselves. Some responses will be better than others, but again the purpose is to sensitize rather than to train a test-writing professional. Most of this chapter is very appropriate for in-class group activities.

3.   Use segments of the television game show "Who Wants To Be a Millionaire?" to demonstrate test taking skills such as self-talk, process of elimination, repeating the question, etc. A keyword search at www.youtube.com will turn up some good clips from which to choose.

Incorporating MRL: Guide students to the Tests and Exams section of the Pearson Study Skills Web site in MRL for additional information and practice.

Reading Workshop Tip: Authors generally have to conduct a great amount of background research in writing their novels to make them more realistic and accurate. Engage students in a discussion of how this research not only contributes to a better understanding of the novel but to their schemata as well. Have them journal about how their novels are helping them build schemata and discuss specific examples of things they learned from their novels that they did not know before.

TAKING STANDARDIZED TESTS

- **READ TO COMPREHEND**

- **INTERACT**

- **ANTICIPATE**

- **RELAX**

- **READ TO LEARN**

- **RECALL**

MAJOR QUESTION TYPES

Main Idea:

- The best statement of the main idea is...

- The best title for this passage is...

- The author is primarily concerned with...

- The central theme of the message is...

Detail:

- The author states that...

- According to the author...

- According to the passage...

- All of the following are true except...

- A person, term, or place is...

Inference:

- The author believes (or feels or implies)...

- It can be inferred from the passage that...

- The passage suggests...

- It can be concluded from the passage that...

Purpose:

- The primary purpose of the passage is...

- The author's purpose is...

Vocabulary: As used in the passage, the best definition...

Reader's Tip
Types of Test Passages

Factual Passages

    What? Science, sociology, psychology or history articles

    How to read? Read for the main idea, and do not get bogged down in details. Remember, you can look back.

    Author's Purpose?

- To inform
- To explain
- To describe

Example: Textbooks

Opinion Passages

    What? Articles with a particular point of view on a topic.

    How to read? Read to determine the author's opinion on the subject. Then judge the value of the support included, and decide whether you agree or disagree.

    Author's Purpose?

- To argue
- To persuade
- To condemn
- To ridicule

Examples: Newspaper editorials

Fiction Passages

    What? Articles that tell a story

    How to Read? Read to understand what the characters are thinking and why they act as they do.

    Author's Purpose?

- To entertain
- To narrate
- To describe
- To shock

Examples: Novels and short stories

75

Reader's Tip
Remembering Information

- Hook it to mental signs that are easy to remember.
- Link it to other information or indicators you already know.
- Sense it by touching, writing, or speaking.
- Rehearse it by writing it or speaking it to yourself.

CHAPTER 7 VOCABULARY LESSON QUIZ

Choose the best word from the list as a synonym for the italicized word.

| memoir | souvenirs | emissary | exclaimed | emitted |
| remit | memorandum | proclamation | clamor | commemorate |

_____ 1. The principal demanded to know the cause of the loud *raucousness* in the cafeteria.

_____ 2. Fireworks are displayed across the country to *honor* Independence Day.

_____ 3. He *shouted* excitedly when he read his college acceptance letter.

_____ 4. The pink lotion *released* the scent of roses.

_____ 5. A popular old saying states that one should not shoot the *messenger* of bad news.

_____ 6. The house foreclosed due to the homeowner's inability to *pay* the mortgage loan.

_____ 7. The beachfront shop contained a variety of *mementos* from sailing trips to Caribbean islands.

_____ 8. An official *note* to all employees outlined the company's new dress-code policies.

_____ 9. Keeping a *diary* to record significant events in life helps in writing an autobiography.

_____ 10. We learned that the old mansion was going to be auctioned off through an *announcement* in the local newspaper.

---

1. clamor 2. commemorate 3. exclaimed 4. emitted 5. emissary
6. remit 7. souvenirs 8. memorandum 9. memoir 10. proclamation

Answer with T *(true) or* F *(false).*

F   _____ 11. *Missiles* are no longer used in military conflicts.

F   _____ 12. Punctual people are likely to be *remiss*.

T   _____ 13. Washington, D.C. has many *memorials* for events and people.

T   _____ 14. Since they could not win as many games, the Chicago Bulls were unable to *reclaim* the championship immediately following Michael Jordan's retirement.

T   _____ 15. Works of fiction sometimes contain *disclaimers* about the characters and conversations presented in the work.

T   _____ 16. Drivers who are caught speeding must *submit* their licenses if requested by the police.

F   _____ 17. Damaged antiques appreciate when they are *irreclaimable*.

T   _____ 18. If a *claimant* waits too long to file an insurance claim, the claim may not be covered.

T   _____ 19. Photographs help capture *memorable* events such as graduations and weddings.

T   _____ 20. *Memorabilia* to some may be junk to others.

Efficient Reading

The emphasis of this text is not on speed but on comprehension. In general, however, students tend to enjoy and profit from a little instruction in efficient reading techniques. You can determine how fast or slowly your students are reading by giving a timed test. A student who is reading easy material at 150 words per minute will have trouble reading college textbooks. Such a student needs to make an effort to read faster.

Chapter Objectives:
- What is your reading rate?
- How fast should you read?
- How can you increase your reading speed?

Transparency Masters:
8.1   Increase Reading Speed
8.2   Reader's Tips: *Managing Workplace Reading* and *Reading Newsletters*

Suggested Teaching Activities:
1.   In introducing efficient reading techniques, help students put speed into perspective. Explain reading flexibility and discuss various materials and purposes that require different reading speeds. Caution students to be sure that they understand that you are not advocating speed reading a biology or history textbook for a final exam.
2.   The exercises on word recognition, word meaning, and phrase meaning are included primarily because they are fun to do and encourage quick thinking. Students enjoy doing them as a group and competing against one another, so consider using them as a class activity. In addition, timing an exercise is easier for the student if the instructor is calling out the time. Do this by calling out *start* and then the number of seconds in five-second intervals. When

everyone is finished, discuss the answers, and then encourage the fast readers and the slow ones. There is no correct speed, but the following would be considered good:

Exercise 2	Word Recognition	40 seconds per list
Exercise 3	Word Meaning	60 seconds per list
Exercise 4	Phrase Meaning	40 seconds per list
Exercise 5	Pen as a Pacer	
	Natural Gas Safety	20 seconds
	Netiquette	25 seconds
	Typing Keyboard	30 seconds
	I Have a Sense of Humor	35 seconds
	Where Are the Women?	60 seconds

Remember, these speeds have no magical meaning. An appropriate speed is individual. It also depends on how often the student is correct. The exercises were designed to be fun and to focus attention on concentration and faster thinking. Use them to have a good time.

3.   Using a pen as a pacer may be awkward at first for many students, but encourage them to try it. Again, doing the exercises in class can make them more fun and also gives students an opportunity to try a new technique with the supervision of the instructor.

4.   If regressions seem to be problematic for students while they read, ask them to try covering the text as they read so they cannot go back.

Incorporating MRL: Guide students to the Reading Rate section of the Pearson Study Skills Web site in MRL and the activities in the Web Resources there. Some are even interactive.

Reading Workshop Tip: After practicing with the exercises in the chapter, have students journal their personal observations regarding their progress as they worked through the activities.

Increase Reading Speed

- **Be Aggressive**
  Actively attack the material.

- **Concentrate**
  Take rest breaks.
  Reward yourself.
  Limit external and internal distractions.
  Visualize.

- **Stop Regressions**
  Be alert on the first reading.

- **Expand Fixations**
  Read phrases or thought units.

- **Use Pen as Pacer**
  Physically pull your eyes down the page.

- **Preview before Reading**
  Establish purpose and activate schema.

- **Set a Time Goal for an Assignment**
  Set a goal and try to meet it.

- **Be Flexible**
  Adjust speed to purpose.

- **Practice**
  "Wishing" vs. "Willing"

Reader's Tip
Managing Workplace Reading

- Set priorities before reading.

- Strive to handle a piece of paper only once.

- Respond to it, discard it, or file it.

Reader's Tip
Reading Newsletters

- Read selectively. You may want to read all of the newsletter or none of it.

- Read critically. You cannot consider the information in a newsletter to be objective since it contains information that is beneficial only to the company or organization. Unflattering information is not included, so the coverage is not balanced.

- Note items that are highlighted, set off by numbers, bullets, capital letters, or appear in boldface or italic type.

Chapter Nine

Analytical Reasoning

This chapter should be fun for the students while encouraging them to think. Discuss the characteristics of successful and unsuccessful students and emphasize the need to persistently and systematically work toward a problem's solution. Discuss how these characteristics apply to reading a textbook and to taking a test. Mention other test-taking clues that you have found helpful.

Chapter Objectives:
- What is good thinking?
- What are the characteristics of unsuccessful students?
- What are the characteristics of successful students?
- What is involved in good problem solving?
- How do graphic illustrations condense complex information?

Transparency Masters:
9.1   Reader's Tips: *Thinking about Maps, Charts, Graphs, and Diagrams* and *Reading and Studying Sociology*
9.2   Reader's Tip: *Evaluating a Credit Card Offer*

Suggested Teaching Activities:
1.   Students will enjoy working together in the introductory exercises. If they want more of these kinds of exercises, refer them to *Problem Solving and Comprehension* by Arthur Whimbey and Jack Lockhead (Philadelphia: Franklin Press, 1980).
2.   A simple Google search for problem solving activities will take you to sites such as Wilderdom (http://wilderdom.com/games/InitiativeGames.html) where several fun interactive problem solving activities can be found.

3.   Often magazines such as *Newsweek* will have feature articles with several graphic aids. Without reading the article, have students analyze the various charts and graphs from an article and summarize the information. Encourage students to make inferences and draw conclusions from the information in the graphics. Finally, read the article together and discuss the use of the graphics information in the article.

Incorporating MRL: Assign students a research topic of interest that indicates a problem such as high gas prices, road rage, the economy, etc. and send them to Research Navigator in MRL. Explain that they will need to locate research for analyzing and solving their research problem. Have them complete the chart that follows which walks them through an analysis from proof that a problem exists, identifying its causes and effects and locating solutions.

Reading Workshop Tip: The type of reading that students will be doing in the above MRL activity, as you know, is very different from the type of reading students do when pleasure reading. Have students journal about the differences they notice between reading for information or research purposes and reading for pleasure.

Research Chart

		Source:
Part I: Showing a problem exists		(use author/s' last name/s or a "keyword" or two from the article title)
A. Fact / Statistic		
B. Fact / Statistic		
Part II: Causes of the Problem		
A. Cause 1		
B. Cause 2 (must have at least two causes)		
C. Cause 3		
Part III: Effects of the Problem		
A. Effect 1		
B. Effect 2 (must have at least two effects)		
C. Effect 3		
Part IV: Solutions to the Problem		
A. Solution 1		
B. Solution 2		

(Chart accompanies *Incorporating MRL* activity)

Reader's Tip
Thinking about Maps, Charts, Graphs, and Diagrams

1. Read the title to determine the subject.
2. Read any information in italics or boldface.
3. Read the footnotes to determine the source of the information.
4. Read the labels to determine what each mark, arrow, figure, or design means.
5. Figure out the *legend*, the key on a map that shows what the markings represent.
6. Notice numbers indicating units of measurement, such as percentages, dollars, thousands, millions, or billions.
7. Notice the trends and extremes. What is the average, and what are the highs and lows?
8. Refer back and forth to the text to follow a process or label parts.
9. Draw conclusions based on the information.
10. Do not read more into the illustration than is supported by fact. In other words, don't draw conclusions that cannot be proved.

Reader's Tip
Reading and Studying Sociology

- Think broadly about society and social organizations. Search for the historical reasons for human behavior and organizational structures. Make cause-and-effect connections between history, culture, and social organizations.
- Compare and contrast customs and social behaviors across cultures.
- Remain open-minded and be tolerant of cultural differences. Avoid biased value judgments.
- Think objectively and scientifically to evaluate the problems of society.

Reader's Tip

Evaluating a Credit Card Offer

- How much is the annual fee for the card?
- What is the finance charge rate? Annual rates typically run 18%–22%, so finance charges can add up quickly.
- Does the rate start low and change after an initial introductory period? The balance may be subject to a higher interest rate after the initial period at the low rate expires.
- Why do you need it? If you already have one card, why do you need another one?

SELECTION 1: PROFILE OF A HURRICANE *Answer with* T *(true) or* F *(false).*

Comprehension Quiz (for prereading or postreading)

F   ___   1. The word *hurricane* is derived from the Hawaiian god of water.

F   ___   2. Typhoons are more like tornadoes than hurricanes.

F   ___   3. According to the passage, most tropical disturbances reach hurricane status.

T   ___   4. From the outside to the center of a hurricane, the barometric pressure drops.

T   ___   5. The eye of the hurricane is the warmest part of the storm.

T   ___   6. The eye of the hurricane is the calmest part of the storm.

F   ___   7. Warm air decreases the strength of a hurricane.

F   ___   8. Hurricanes usually build strength as they move across land.

T   ___   9. Cold ocean waters decrease hurricane strength.

F   ___   10. A storm surge refers to the wind from a hurricane.

Vocabulary Quiz (for prereading or postreading)

F   ___   1. A *tranquil* evening is characterized by violence.

T   ___   2. A ceiling fan cools by a *rotary* movement.

T   ___   3. Sleet is a form of *precipitation*.

T   ___   4. A basketball player can benefit from *deceptive* moves on the court.

F   ___   5. *Liberated* criminals report to jail for imprisonment.

T   ___   6. Look *aloft* to see clouds or stars.

F   ___   7. A *barrage* of ammunition is a single deadly shot.

F   ___   8. A scheduled airplane departure is an example of flying *debris*.

T   ___   9. *Torrential* rains are rains that are heavier than usual.

T   ___   10. The *advent* of a holiday season is the beginning rather than the end.

SELECTION 2: GENDER AND SOCIAL INSTITUTIONS

Answer with T *(true) or* F *(false).*

Comprehension Quiz (for prereading or postreading)

T   _____   1. Research shows that in general marriage improves health and raises income.

T   _____   2. Studies show that divorced women are happier than divorced men.

T   _____   3. More than half of all college students are now women.

T   _____   4. Researcher Jessie Bernard claims that it is unhealthy for women to be saddled with most of the housework in a marriage.

F   _____   5. According to the passage, research on ads reveals that men and women are equally shown lying on sofas or beds.

T   _____   6. When television became popular in the 1950s, men had almost all the starring roles.

F   _____   7. Our society tends to label jobs requiring endurance as "feminine jobs."

T   _____   8. In the early years of television, advertisers targeted women during the day because so many woman were at-home wives.

T   _____   9. Women have been part of the military since the Revolutionary War.

T   _____   10. A century ago in the U.S. most people did not think women should work for pay.

Vocabulary Quiz (for prereading or postreading)

F   _____   1. A *humdrum* routine usually suggests that life is boring rather than exciting.

T   _____   2. *Conventional* wisdom suggests knowledge that is commonly accepted.

T   _____   3. The *stereotype* of a corporate executive is a leader with money and power.

T   _____   4. A parent who always favors one child over another is guilty of *bias*.

T   _____   5. The banning of *inappropriate* books is permissible in private school libraries.

T   _____   6. For some sporting events, spectators have seats *indicated* by numbers.

F   _____   7. A *subtle* message is stated directly and fully explained.

T   _____   8. A student shows *competence* in a subject by passing the tests.

F   _____   9. The look of a smile and a *pout* are about the same to an observer.

T   _____   10. A *rural* area is less populated than an urban area.

SELECTION 3: MOTIVATING YOURSELF

Answer with T *(true) or* F *(false).*

Comprehension Quiz (for prereading or postreading)

F _____ 1. The author would agree that motivation should come from the supervisor.

T _____ 2. Maltz was a plastic surgeon who observed positive changes in his patients after surgery.

T _____ 3. Self-fulfillment is the highest level on Maslow's hierarchy of needs.

T _____ 4. Gellerman believes that you should work for the organization and yourself at the same time.

T _____ 5. It is implied that motivation-seekers usually achieve more than maintenance-seekers.

Vocabulary Quiz (for prereading or postreading)

T _____ 1. Too much supervision can make an employee feel *stifled*.

T _____ 2. An *inspired* worker wants to achieve a goal.

F _____ 3. The *proponent* of a cause is firmly against it.

T _____ 4. If you operate on a *premise*, you have some basis for drawing conclusions.

T _____ 5. To reach the *pinnacle* of success is considered the highest level of achievement.

F _____ 6. The *crux* of an issue is an insignificant detail.

T _____ 7. A *de-emphasis* on college language study would probably mean fewer language requirements for graduation.

F _____ 8. A sociologist is primarily concerned with personal *hygiene*.

T _____ 9. *Grievances* are complaints that are made by workers.

T _____ 10. *Verbalizing* a problem can be a way of relieving tension.

SELECTION 3: MOTIVATING YOURSELF ACTIVITY

ANALYTICAL REASONING: APPLICATION OF A NEW SKILL

SUGGESTED RESPONSE: The author would support the first four options. The remaining six offer very little. Some, in fact, could do more harm than good.

Norman works for a company that has many advantages. He might not improve his situation elsewhere. His first step, therefore, is to motivate himself. If his attitude improves, he will be more likely to be considered for a better role. Norman should then talk with his supervisor about assuming more responsibility. He might get some assistance, perhaps psychological support, from a discussion with the right person.

When an employee becomes dissatisfied or reaches a plateau it is always a good idea to search for a role with another company. There are two reasons for this: (1) the individual can thus find out whether or not he (or she) can really improve himself—instead of just thinking about it—and (2) searching for a better role often motivates the person in his present job because it helps him get out of a mental rut. It can also make him see more clearly the advantages (or disadvantages) of his present job.

CHAPTER 9 VOCABULARY LESSON QUIZ

Answer with T *(true) or* F *(false).*

T ____ 1. A well-read person is likely to be *conversant* on many topics.

F ____ 2. *Versatile* gymnasts have difficulty moving from one exercise to another.

T ____ 3. An *introverted* lawyer may feel less comfortable than an extroverted attorney in presenting cases before a jury and a packed courtroom.

F ____ 4. Compact discs can be removed from CD players by pushing the *deject* button.

T ____ 5. The Census Bureau *projects* that the population drawing Social Security will increase as baby boomers retire and apply for benefits.

T ____ 6. Songs are composed of several *verses.*

T ____ 7. The Catholic Church prefers that non-Catholics *convert* before marrying a Catholic.

T ____ 8. *Diversion* programs are used to steer high-risk youth away from trouble and failure.

T ____ 9. Travelers who are prone to *vertigo* should avoid taking cruises on small vessels.

F ____ 10. Loyal friends interact with one another *subversively.*

Choose the best word from the list to complete the following sentences.

version	reverted	abject	extroverted	ejected
conjecture	ambivert	adjacent	interjecting	injected

_____ 11. Despite appearances, not all entertainers are _____; many are actually quite shy off-stage.

_____ 12. Reporters are notorious for _____ questions during press conferences.

_____ 13. To be prepared for messages, it is convenient to keep a pencil and pad _____ to the phone.

_____ 14. The toddler threw away her pacifier and _____ back to sucking her thumb.

_____ 15. The ideal professor is an _____, and is comfortable with both introspective activities as well as teaching classes.

_____ 16. Some citizens feel that for decades public housing concentrated the poor in _____ poverty.

_____ 17. The nurse carefully _____ the needle into the patient's arm.

_____ 18. Having been _____ from the game by the referee, the angry player stormed off the court.

_____ 19. Since there was little evidence on which to base his theory, the detective's opinion about the murder was merely _____.

_____ 20. The recently updated _____ of *Psycho* was just as chilling as the original movie.

---

11. extroverted 12. interjecting 13. adjacent 14. reverted 15. ambivert
16. abject 17. injected 18. ejected 19. conjecture 20. version

Inference

As you present Chapter Ten, keep in mind that students probably have a better understanding of the word 'imply' than they do the word 'infer.' Spend some time getting them to see that imply and infer mean the same thing; it just depends on whether the message is being sent or received. Explain to students that speakers and writers imply meaning in the messages they are sending, and listeners and readers infer meaning from the messages they receive.

Chapter Objectives:
- What is implied meaning?
- Why would meaning be implied rather than stated directly?
- What is slanted language or connotation of words?
- What kinds of clues imply meaning?
- How do good readers draw conclusions?

Transparency Masters:
10.1   Inference Activity (#3 below): Using Positive Connotation for Political Spin
10.2   Reader's Tip: *Reading Editorials*

Suggested Teaching Activities:

1.   Cartoons (political as well as humorous) are great tools for teaching inferences. They graphically illustrate to students the importance of background knowledge in gaining meaning. Look at a few of these with your students and model the thinking processes that you go through as you begin to 'get it'. Have students bring in some favorite cartoons and explain to their classmates why these particular cartoons are favorites. Usually, implied meaning is the reason the cartoons are well-liked.

2.   Jokes are another tool to use when teaching inferences. Ask students how many times after hearing a joke that they or someone they know said, "I don't get it," or "That's not funny," only to laugh when it has been explained to them. Chances are that the person who 'didn't get it' missed something that was implied in the joke's setup. Another way to look at it is by watching the person who is slow to see the humor in the joke and says, minutes later, "Oh, I get it!" Usually it is something that is implied that finally occurs to this person.

3.   Sensitize students to the political manipulation of phrases with a positive connotation. Ask students to write a speech stating a position on an issue and using the phrases on Transparency Master 10.1. Discuss the familiarity of the phrases and the impact. Ask questions such as why politicians use such phrases? How effective are they?

4.   Stress to students that they already use inferential comprehension skills in everyday life. Scenarios help students to understand what it means to infer meaning. Present the following scenarios as examples of inferring and come up with a few of your own. Students can probably contribute some of these as well.

- Have you ever awoken in the morning and reached over to touch the window even before getting out of bed? What were you doing?
- When a friend wants you to go on a blind date, you ask what the person looks like. Your friend responds, "He/She has a great personality!" What do you think?

Incorporating MRL: Guide students to the Critical Thinking section of the Pearson Study Skills Web site located in MRL. There they will find activities and additional Web Resources for more practice making inferences.

Reading Workshop Tip: Authors rely on readers to make inferences while they read. Have students journal about some of the inferences they have made during their reading.

Using Positive Connotation for Political Spin

(Inference Assignment)

Create a political speech stating your position on a national issue. Weave the following phrases into your speech:

New attitude

Bet on the future

Strengthen the American family

Empower Americans to make decisions for their own lives

Right choice for the country

New approach for America

Important moment for the country

How America is meant to be

Good sound judgment for the people

Come together and do what is right for the people

Reader's Tip
Reading Editorials

- What event prompted the editorial?
- What is the thesis or opinion being promoted by the author?
- Do the details prove the thesis?
- Is the author liberal or conservative?
- What is left out?
- Are the sources, facts, and other support credible?

SELECTION 1: THE BEST PLACE

Answer with T *(true) or* F *(false).*

Comprehension Quiz (for prereading or postreading)

T   ____   1. Tom Campbell always seemed to have trouble remembering Dr. Whitney's name.

F   ____   2. Henry Hammond was captured at the Mexican border.

F   ____   3. Henry Hammond was convicted of armed robbery.

F   ____   4. Tom Campbell questioned why Dr. Whitney remained in his position as prison physician.

F   ____   5. Tom Campbell turned down two promotions because he was not offered a raise to go with the extra work.

T   ____   6. Dr. Whitney waited until all the staff were on coffee break and then called for Henry Hammond.

T   ____   7. Dr. Whitney used a blood pressure reading to trick Henry Hammond.

F   ____   8. Dr. Whitney's parents were also medical physicians.

T   ____   9. Dr. Whitney hypnotized Henry Hammond to learn of the bank account numbers where the money was stashed.

T   ____   10. Dr. Whitney used his job at the infirmary to carry out criminal activity.

Vocabulary Quiz (for prereading or postreading)

T   ____   1. If the motorcycle were *deceptively* new looking, it probably had been used previously.

T   ____   2. A smile or a wink can *acknowledge* the entrance of a new person into the room.

T   ____   3. One punishment for illegal immigration is *extradition* to the country of origin.

F   ____   4. In order to understand behavior, a *financier* is required to have a degree in psychology.

T   ____   5. Kids who do not want to go to bed attempt various *manipulations* to extend bedtime.

F   ____   6. *Stashed* money is probably not put in a place that you think is safe.

T   ____   7. Loud music can be *distracting* for students who are studying.

F   ____   8. A *limp* body is toned, tight, and ready for a fight.

T   ____   9. The success of a hypnotist relies largely on the ability to induce a *trance*.

T   ____   10. An *extracted* tooth is no longer growing in the mouth.

SELECTION 2: THE ALCHEMIST'S SECRET

Answer with T *(true) or* F *(false).*

Comprehension Quiz (for prereading or postreading)

T _____ 1. The author implies that Pechkoff, the foreign diplomat, had his first wife killed.

T _____ 2. The wife in the story who eats the chocolates was seeing a younger man and wanted a settlement.

T _____ 3. An autopsy of Pechkoff's wife is done to discover the cause of death.

F _____ 4. The husband and Pechkoff were business partners.

T _____ 5. The wife reached Dr. Maximus before the husband.

SELECTION 3: A DEAL IN DIAMONDS

Answer with T *(true) or* F *(false).*

Comprehension Quiz (for prereading or postreading)

T   _____   1. Pete got the idea of the diamond heist when he saw a girl toss a penny into the plaza fountain.

F   _____   2. Johnny was a good choice as partner in crime because his record was well-known in the east.

F   _____   3. The organizer Johnny was the one who actually snatched the diamonds in the heist.

F   _____   4. Pete had to ask that the window to the diamond office be opened to let in some air.

T   _____   5. The police thought the men were stealing the coins out of the fountain.

Vocabulary Quiz (for prereading or postreading)

F   _____   1. If they *strolled* to the movies, they were running hurriedly through the crowd.

T   _____   2. If the model were a real *fashion-plate*, she would not wear those out-dated jeans.

F   _____   3. *Reluctantly* agreeing is enthusiastically joining with the group.

T   _____   4. Early Saturday morning construction on the sidewalk can be a *disturbance* to sleeping residents.

T   _____   5. A previous *commitment* can be reason to decline a late invitation for the same evening.

T   _____   6. When seeds are scattered by the wind, the resulting flowers are randomly *mingled* together.

F   _____   7. A man in a *dapper* suit is most likely wearing an outdated outfit.

T   _____   8. A lottery winner cannot collect money until the ticket number is *confirmed.*

T   _____   9. You can go *wading* in a pool even if the water is only one foot deep.

F   _____   10. A person who is sent to the *cooler* to await trial is placed under house arrest.

CHAPTER 10 VOCABULARY LESSON QUIZ

Answer the following with correct (C) or incorrect (I).

C   ____   1. The *tenant* had two cats, yet kept a spotless apartment.

C   ____   2. The *gregarious* young woman enjoyed talking at the party and stayed late.

C   ____   3. Not even the experienced plumber could fix the *continuous* drip.

C   ____   4. Kidnapping the child was an *egregious* act that deserved punishment.

C   ____   5. Deep in the forest, we discovered a *secluded* cabin that few could ever find.

I   ____   6. *Discontented* with her new haircut, she thanked the hairdresser and eagerly booked another appointment.

C   ____   7. Her *intent* was to arrive early, but she was still a few minutes late.

C   ____   8. Vultures began to *congregate* over the carcass soon after the deer was killed.

C   ____   9. *Contented*, the children were calm after their afternoon snack and took a nap.

I   ____   10. The *recluse* regularly left her apartment to visit friends, and was often seen at the local diner.

Choose the best word from the list as a synonym for the following:

exclude	untenable	aggregation	inclusive	retain
tenable	perseverance	segregate	preclude	contentment

_____ 11. Keep

_____ 12. Divide

_____ 13. Collection

_____ 14. Prevent

_____ 15. Shut out

_____ 16. Defendable

_____ 17. Tenacity

_____ 18. Satisfaction

_____ 19. Encompassing

_____ 20. Unfathomable

11. retain 12. segregate 13. aggregation 14. preclude 15. exclude
16. tenable 17. perseverance 18. contentment 19. inclusive 20. untenable

Chapter Eleven

Critical Reading

Teaching students to read critically is to teach them to see beyond the printed page. One effective way to introduce this chapter and illustrate the skill of critical thinking is the courtroom analogy. Point out how:

1) attorneys question prospective jurors to uncover bias and to detect attitude through the tone of answers, etc.;

2) attorneys go to great lengths to distinguish fact from opinion when questioning witnesses;

3) juries must examine testimony and evidence and arrive at a verdict. Good jurors take their charge seriously and work diligently to complete their civic duty.

Chapter Objectives:

- What is an author's purpose or intent?
- What is point of view?
- What is bias?
- What is tone?
- How do you distinguish between fact and opinion?
- What are fallacies?

Transparency Masters:

Suggested Teaching Activities:

1.   It would be interesting to have conflicting opinions of a historical figure from two historians as an example.

2.   Newspaper editorials are also useful for teaching critical reading. Collect a few that are funny. Share some of these with your students and talk about how the writers say one thing but mean another. For an assignment, ask students to bring in an editorial and answer the following questions about it:

- **Purpose or intent:** Why did the author write the article?
- **Bias or point of view:** What side does the author take on the subject (for or against)?
- **Main idea (implied meaning):** What point is the author trying to make?
- **Background knowledge:** What do you need to know to understand the editorial?
- **Tone:** What is the feeling or mood of the passage? (examples: sarcastic, angry, sympathetic, humorous)

3.   Advertisements are fun to use when teaching fallacies. Bring in several examples to illustrate the various fallacies. Discuss a few and then see if students can identify some on their own. This is a good group activity.

Incorporating MRL: Send students to the Opinions section of the *New York Times* on the Web in Research Navigator. Have them select an editorial of interest to them and critique it for author's purpose, bias, tone, etc.

Reading Workshop Tip: Critical thinking can be applied to pleasure reading as well. Ask students if they detect a bias on the part of the author in the telling of the story. What is the tone of the book they are reading? Is there an implied point the author is making regarding the subject matter of the book? Does the author appear to take a stand on a controversial topic, for instance? For further explanation, use television shows as examples of entertainment that may also reflect the author's position on a subject.

CRITICAL READERS RECOGNIZE:

The Author's Purpose or Intent

To inform   To persuade   To entertain

The Author's Point of View or Bias

- Writer's opinion or position on topic

- Author's perspective or view

Biases

- Tend to be associated with prejudice

- Author's bias

- Reader's bias

The Author's Tone

- Attitude toward subject

- Relates to tone of voice

Fact and Opinion

- Facts can be proven true or false;

- Opinions are feelings or beliefs that cannot be proven.

Reader's Tip
Recognizing the Author's Tone

The following list of words with explanations can describe an author's tone or attitude:

Absurd, farcical, ridiculous: laughable or a joke

Ambivalent, apathetic, detached: not caring

Angry, bitter, hateful: feeling bad and upset about the topic

Arrogant, condescending: acting conceited or above others

Awestruck, admiring, wondering: filled with wonder

Cheerful, joyous, happy: feeling good about the topic

Compassionate, sympathetic: feeling sorrow at the distress of others

Complex: intricate, complicated, and entangled with confusing parts

Congratulatory, celebratory: honoring an achievement or festive occasion

Cruel, malicious: meanspirited

Cynical: expecting the worst from people

Depressed, melancholy: sad, dejected, or having low spirits

Disapproving: judging unfavorably

Distressed: suffering strain, misery, or agony

Evasive, abstruse: avoiding or confusing the issue

Formal: using an official style

Frustrated: blocked from a goal

Gentle: kind or of a high social class

Ghoulish, grim: robbing graves or feeding on corpses; stern and forbidding

Hard: unfeeling, strict, and unrelenting

Humorous, jovial, comic, playful, amused: being funny

Incredulous: unbelieving

Indignant: outraged

Intense, impassioned: extremely involved, zealous, or agitated

Ironic: the opposite of what is expected; a twist at the end

Irreverent: lack of respect for authority

Mocking, scornful, caustic, condemning: ridiculing the topic

Objective, factual, straightforward, critical: using facts without emotions

(Continued on next page)

Obsequious: fawning for attention

Optimistic: looking on the bright side

Outspoken: speaking one's mind on issues

Pathetic: moving one to compassion or pity

Pessimistic: looking on the negative side

Prayerful: religiously thankful

Reticent: shy and not speaking out

Reverent: showing respect

Righteous: morally correct

Romantic, intimate, loving: expressing love or affection

Sarcastic: saying one thing and meaning another

Satiric: using irony, wit, and sarcasm to discredit or ridicule

Sensational: overdramatized or overhyped

Sentimental, nostalgic: remembering the good old days

Serious, sincere, earnest, solemn: being honest and concerned

Straightforward: forthright

Subjective, opinionated: expressing opinions and feelings

Tragic: regrettable or deplorable mistake

Uneasy: restless or uncertain

Vindictive: seeking revenge

Common Fallacies

Testimonials: Celebrities who are not experts state support.

Example: Tiger Woods appears in television advertisements endorsing a particular credit card.

Bandwagon: You will be left out if you do not join the crowd.

Example: All the voters in the district support Henson for senator.

Transfer: A famous person is associated with an argument.

Example: George Washington indicated in a quote that he would have agreed with us on this issue.

Straw Person: A simplistic exaggeration is set up to represent the argument.

Example: The professor replied, "If I delay the exam, you'll expect me to change the due dates of all papers and assignments."

Misleading Analogy: Two things are compared as similar that are actually distinctly different.

Example: Studying is like taking a shower; most of the material goes down the drain.

Circular Reasoning: The conclusion is supported by restating it.

Example: Papers must be turned in on time because papers cannot be turned in late.

Reader's Tip

Critically Evaluating Electronic Material

Ask the following questions to evaluate:

- What are the author's credentials in the field? Is the author affiliated with a university? Check this by noting professional titles in the preface or introduction, finding a biographical reference in the library, or searching the Internet for additional references to the same author.
- Who paid for the Web page? Check the home page for an address. Does the electronic address end in *edu, gov, org,* or *com*? Depending on the material, this sponsor could lend credibility or raise further questions.
- What is the purpose of the Web page? Is the purpose to educate or to sell a product, a service, or an idea? Check the links to investigate any hidden agendas.
- How do the biases of the author and the sponsor affect the material? Is the reasoning sound? Check the tone, assumptions, and evidence. What opposing views have been left out?

Selection 1: The Dinner Party

Answer with T *(true) or* F *(false).*

Comprehension Quiz (for prereading or postreading)

F   _____   1. The American naturalist is the brother of Mrs. Wynnes.

F   _____   2. The young girl at the party is the colonel's daughter.

F   _____   3. Mrs. Wynnes sees the snake go under the table.

T   _____   4. The colonel is outspoken in stereotyping the reactions of women.

F   _____   5. Mrs. Wynnes orders raw meat to lure the snake from the guests.

Vocabulary Quiz (for prereading or postreading)

T   _____   1. *Colonial* officials lived in countries ruled by the British Empire.

T   _____   2. *Attachés* serve government diplomats in foreign embassies.

T   _____   3. A *naturalist* studies both plants and animals.

F   _____   4. A *spacious* closet provides little room for clothes.

T   _____   5. Skin *contracts* when you enter cold ocean water.

T   _____   6. To *summon* a taxi is to call for transportation.

F   _____   7. A *veranda* is a glass-enclosed room with plants.

T   _____   8. As an object flies towards the eye, an initial *impulse* is to blink.

T   _____   9. Starting a *commotion* can distract a security guard's concentration.

T   _____ 10. To *forfeit* a game is to offer a victory to your opponent.

SELECTION 2: LET'S TELL THE STORY OF ALL AMERICA'S CULTURES

Answer with T *(true) or* F *(false).*

Comprehension Quiz (for prereading or postreading)

F   _____   1. Nat Turner was one of the heroes in the author's history books.

T   _____   2. The author educated himself on the contributions of immigrants to America's history.

F   _____   3. Educators have long recognized that America has a long history of multi-cultural contributions to democratic ideals.

F   _____   4. Several dissenting members of the New York committee argue that the report puts the focus on national unity and not ethnicity.

T   _____   5. The author believes it is the diversity that built America that contributes to its uniqueness.

Vocabulary Quiz (for prereading or postreading)

T   _____   1. Many argue that it was the *industrialists* of the early 19th century that brought America to its greatness.

T   _____   2. Many early pioneers feared traveling westward due to rumors of *scalpers*.

F   _____   3. The old Labrador retriever *adapted* the abandoned cub as her own.

F   _____   4. *Abolitionists* are people who oppose government.

T   _____   **5.** The *migration* of the birds from Mexico has been disrupted by recent hurricane activity in the Gulf of Mexico.

F   _____   6. *Indigenous* people are often considered very smart.

T   _____   7. The *inconsistencies* in the two witness' testimony caused the jury to be skeptical.

T   _____   8. *Dissenting* members of Congress have been known to boycott sessions.

F   _____   9. *Ethnicity*, or the drive to do the right thing, is often neglected in the workplace.

T   _____   10. The coach's pep talk at half time did not succeed in *bolstering* the team's spirit.

SELECTION 3: WE'LL GO FORWARD FROM THIS MOMENT

Answer with T *(true) or* F *(false).*

Comprehension Quiz (for prereading or postreading)

T _____ 1. The author suggests that Americans are spoiled.

T _____ 2. The author suggests that Americans sometimes quarrel among themselves.

T _____ 3. The author suggests that the terrorists probably think that Americans are weak.

F _____ 4. The author refers to a book that he has written about the American spirit.

T _____ 5. The author believes that Americans will rally together against the terrorists.

Vocabulary Quiz (for prereading or postreading)

F _____ 1. To *steel* your nerves is to resign yourself to weakness.

T _____ 2. *Frivolous* children enjoy carefree play.

T _____ 3. To use time wisely, corporate executives should delegate some *minutiae* to staffers.

F _____ 4. A *blithe* spirit is heavy with sorrow.

T _____ 5. An *entitlement* is a right that we somehow think we deserve.

F _____ 6. *Grappling* with an infection means you have defeated the disease.

T _____ 7. A *recrimination* directs blame at a deserving culprit.

F _____ 8. To *chasten* a leader is to appoint her to a significant office.

F _____ 9. A *bickering* family agrees without disagreeing.

T _____ 10. To *cherish* your childhood memories is to value your early experiences.

CHAPTER 11 VOCABULARY LESSON QUIZ

Answer with T (true) or F (false).

T   _____   1. The Harlem *Renaissance* was an explosion or rebirth of art and literature in Harlem.

F   _____   2. The country in which you live always determines your legal *nationality*.

F   _____   3. Children usually dislike listening to readers who use *inflection* in their voice.

T   _____   4. Ballerinas are able to *flex* their bodies gracefully.

T   _____   5. When appropriate, responsible journalists try to *incorporate* factual evidence from credible sources into their articles.

T   _____   6. Surgical procedures are sometimes used by *corpulent* people to lose weight.

F   _____   7. Tropical flowers are *native* to the Great Plains of the Midwest.

F   _____   8. Being polite is most likely an *innate* rather than a learned quality.

F   _____   9. *Corpuscles* are fat cells that store energy for later use.

T   _____   10. In some churches, it is customary to *genuflect* before or during the service.

Choose the best word from the list to complete the following sentences.

corpse	reflective	corporal	reflector	reflect
deflect	naturalized	corporation	naïve	corps

_____ 11. The _____ diner did not know which fork to use for his salad.

_____ 12. Due to security concerns, it may become increasingly difficult for foreign-born individuals to become _____ citizens.

_____ 13. The Army _____ of Engineers is relied upon to update flood maps.

_____ 14. Yoga participants are encouraged to _____ as they exercise in order to relax their minds as well as bodies.

_____ 15. A judge is likely to become annoyed with witnesses who attempt to _____ questions rather than directly answer them.

_____ 16. It is not uncommon for similar businesses to join together and form a large _____.

_____ 17. The _____ was examined by the local coroner in order to report on cause of death.

_____ 18. Place a _____ on your bike if you ride after dark so that drivers can spot you.

_____ 19. _____ punishment is a controversial form of discipline that is outlawed in many European countries.

_____ 20. The _____ writer enjoyed weaving her thoughts into sensitive poetry.

11. naïve 12. naturalized 13. Corps 14. reflect 15. deflect
16. corporation 17. corpse 18. reflector 19. corporal 20. reflective

Introduction to Full-length Chapter Selection

The ultimate goal of this text is for students to transfer the reading skills and strategies they have learned to other courses and material. The chapter-length selection in this appendix is intended as a smaller scale practice of this goal.

You will notice that the textbook selection comes without the ordinary previewing questions and activities accompanying the other longer reading passages in the book.

Remind students that although this chapter (and others to come later during their college years) does not have the traditional *I think this will tell me _____*, they still need to remember and apply the previewing strategies they have learned and practiced throughout your course.

This chapter, like those from other discipline-specific texts, does have its own type of preview questions, as well as comprehension checks scattered at various points. Help your students realize that these questions form the basis for activating their schemata and monitoring their comprehension, just as the typical *Breaking Through* questions do. Remember to draw their attention to the material provided in the graphics, photos, and inserts placed within the chapter.

Encourage students to apply the six strategies of good readers throughout the chapter-length selection. Suggest that the more they interact with it, the better their comprehension and test performance is likely to be. Reading the chapter is a start, annotating better, and note taking probably the best way to increase involvement and knowledge.

As in the independent textbook assignment, you will find that the exam for the chapter-length selection includes both multiple choice, true-false, and essay questions. Since some of the questions refer to graphics and inserts in the chapter, you will want to specifically review for these items or possibly use the objective portion as a take-home or open book test. You are the expert on your class; adapt the exam to allow your students to demonstrate what they have learned.

Objective Exam

Answer the following with a, b, c, or d.

b _____ 1. The author indicates that

    a. hard-working individuals can accomplish more than groups.

    b. most goals and tasks are accomplished within a group structure.

    c. goals are achieved equally well by both individuals and groups.

    d. groups with leaders tend to accomplish more than individuals working alone.

c _____ 2. According to the author, leaders practice all of the following *except*

    a. inspiring.

    b. modeling.

    c. searching.

    d. challenging.

a _____ 3. The selection includes a list from the U.S. Guidebook for Marines to

    a. show examples of valued military leadership characteristics.

    b. demonstrate that excellent leaders possess each of the qualities listed.

    c. explain what qualifies a soldier to become an officer in the Marine Corps.

    d. provide a way to measure leadership qualities in civilians.

d _____ 4. The author states that there are two types of leadership,

    a. transformational and interactional.

    b. transactional and charismatic.

    c. transactional and individual.

    d. transactional and transformational.

c _____ 5. The author believes that powerful business leaders and public service leaders

    a. typically come from wealthy families.

    b. have in most cases inherited their leadership positions.

    c. share a number of common traits.

    d. have strong support.

b _____ 6. The selection states that "Middle managers are akin to department heads." The best meaning of the word *akin* is:

    a. undependable.

    b. similar.

    c. secondary.

    d. reporting.

d _____ 7. All of the following phrases from the selection have positive connotations *except*

    a. select the best.

    b. empower employees.

    c. enhance career development.

    d. bogged down with meetings.

b _____ 8. The author refers to Dr. Martin Luther King, Jr. as

    a. an example of a transactional leader.

    b. an example of a transformational leader.

    c. an example of a man who demonstrates each of the U.S. Marine Corps leadership traits.

    d. an example of a man who was able to weave together individual and corporate interests.

c _____ 9. According to the selection, frontline managers

    a. operate between the middle management and top management levels.

    b. are responsible for establishing goals and the strategies to meet them.

    c. are also known as supervisors.

    d. are also known as department heads.

a _____ 10. The author suggests that using Mickey Mouse to entertain guests waiting in line at Disney parks is an example of

    a. creative management.

    b. the decision making function of management.

    c. transactional leadership.

    d. transformational leadership.

Answer the following with T *(true) or* F *(false).*

F _____ 11. Issadore Sharp started the Marriott Hotel chain in Canada.

T _____ 12. Top managers are responsible for making medium to long range plans and for establishing goals and strategies to meet those goals.

F _____ 13. Peter Drucker says that leadership is about popularity.

F _____ 14. Van Eure waited tables at a competing restaurant to learn to operate the Angus Barn.

F _____ 15. William Fisher's essentials for leadership spell the word SUCCESS.

T _____ 16. By "empower employees," the author suggests that the more important people feel, the better they work.

F _____ 17. Marilyn Carlson Nelson is the founder of the Radisson Hotel chain.

T _____ 18. After September 11, 2001, hotel occupancy slumped to single digits.

F _____ 19. The author considers Southwest Airlines' Herb Kelleher to be an outstanding transactional leader because he both empowers and inspires his employees.

F _____ 20. Entertaining business guests at a restaurant would be an example of a manager's negotiator role.

T _____ 21. The selection states that, while effective leaders differ in terms of background, they act similarly.

T _____ 22. The author suggests that former New York mayor Rudolph Giuliani provides an example of an effective leader with such characteristics as a strong ego and an orientation towards the future.

F _____ 23. The management function of controlling refers to a top-level manager making decisions for the lower and middle level managers.

T _____ 24. A manager of a fast-food restaurant who steps to the counter to help his staff service customers would also be considered a frontline manager.

T _____ 25. Career development can be a two-edged sword because highly trained employees will leave the company for a better job.

Essay Question

1. Compare and contrast the roles of leaders and managers. Include at least one example of each role in your answer.

2. Explain the difference between transactional and transformational leadership. Provide at least one example of each type.

STUDY OUTLINE:
LEADERSHIP AND MANAGEMENT

I. Leadership

   A. Characteristics of leaders (U.S. Guidebook for Marines), page 544

   B. Practices of leaders
     1. Challenge the process
     2. Inspire a shared vision
     3. Enable others to act
     4. Model the way
     5. Encourage the heart

   C. Definitions of leadership, page 544-545

   D. Transactional leadership, page 546
     1. Leader obtains desired actions through behaviors, rewards, incentives
     2. Exchange/transaction between leader and follower

   E. Transformational leadership, page 547
     1. Leader elicits performance beyond the usual level
     2. Three important factors
       a. Charisma
       b. Individual consideration
       c. Intellectual stimulation
     3. Examples of leadership types, page 547
       a. Dr. Martin Luther King, Jr.
       b. Herb Kelleher

   F. William Fisher's focus on leadership, page 549
     1. **L**oyalty
     2. **E**xcellence
     3. **A**ssertiveness
     4. **D**edication
     5. **E**nthusiasm
     6. **R**isk management

7. **S**trength
8. **H**onor
9. **I**nspiration
10. **P**erformance

G. Groups placing demands on leaders, page 550
    1. Owners
    2. Corporate office
    3. Guests
    4. Employees
    5. Regulatory agencies
    6. Competitors

H. Leadership skills with employees, page 552
    1. Be decisive
    2. Follow through
    3. Select the best
    4. Empower employees
    5. Enhance career development

II. Hospitality Management

A. Definition of management, page 553
    1. Efficiency
    2. Effectiveness

B. Levels of management, page 555
    1. Frontline
    2. Middle
    3. Top

C. Functions of management, page 556
    1. Planning
    2. Organizing
    3. Decision making
    4. Communicating
    5. Motivating
    6. Controlling

D. Skills of management, page 556
    1. Conceptual
    2. Interpersonal
    3. Technical

E. Roles of management, page 557
    1. Figurehead
    2. Leader
    3. Liaison
    4. Spokesperson
    5. Negotiator

III. Differences between leading and managing, page 559

A. Leading: a person's vision influences others' behaviors in some desired way

B. Managing: a person achieves objectives through the efforts of subordinates

IV. Ethics, page 560

A. Integral part of hospitality decisions

B. Code of Ethics for the hospitality and tourism industry

C. Ethical dilemmas in hospitality
    1. Kickbacks
    2. Gifts
    3. Bribes

V. Trends in Leadership and Management, p. 562

Reader's Tip
Categorizing Idioms

Idioms are sometimes categorized into the following groups:

- Word families: grouping around a similar individual word

    Down as in *step down, take down, pipe down, narrow down, nail down, run down, tear down, knock down, let down, die down, cut down*

- Verb + Preposition: action word plus a connecting word

    Hammer away means *persist; stand for* means *represent,* and *roll back* means *reduce*

- Preposition + Noun: connecting word plus the name of a person, place, or thing

    On foot means *walking, by heart* means *memorized,* and *off guard* means *surprised.*

- Verb + Adjective: action word plus a descriptive word

    Think twice means *consider carefully, hang loose* means *be calm,* and *play fair* means *deal equally*

- Pairs of Nouns: two words naming a person, place, or thing

    Flesh and blood means *kin, part and parcel* means *total,* and *pins and needles* means *deal equally*

- Pairs of adjectives: two descriptive words

    Cut and dried means *obvious, fair and square* means *honest, short and sweet* means brief.

Reader's Tip
Internet Sites to Explore

Dave's ESL Café www.eslcafe.com/

Emphasis in this site is on English as it is spoken in the United States. It includes search tools for ESL books and a general discussion forum for ESL students and teachers.

EF Englishtown www. englishtown.com

Englishtown is translated into eight languages and has learning games, bulletin boards where you can ask grammar and culture questions, a location for ESL/EFL teachers, a pen pal club, and a school where you can take classes online.

English Club www.Englishclub.com

This site has a 24-hour ESL Help Desk staffed with teachers to answer questions. Resources are available for both instructors and students in areas such as grammar, speech, and reading.

English Zone www.English-Zone.com

This is a site for students who are learning English as a Second Language or studying English in general. It provides instruction and exercises on idioms, verbs, grammar, writing, spelling, vocabulary, and reading.

Tower of English www.towerofenglish.com/

Tower of English allows students to integrate lots of Web sources into their learning experiences. It provides links to online ELS exercises, search engines, reference tools, and news sources.

Vocabulary List for Longer Reading Selections
(by chapter # and selection #)

abolitionist 11.2
abruptly 2.3
acquittal 2.3
acknowledgment 6.1,
10.1
adapted 11.2
advent 9.1
affluent 5.2
alchemist 10.2
aloft 9.1
alluded 2.3
amiss 2.2
annals 5.2
ascribed 4.1
attaches 11.1
auditory 6.3
authentic 4.2
autopsy 5.3, 10.2
avert 6.3
banning 9.2
baser metals 10.2
barrage 9.1
barrier island 2.2
bias 9.2
bickering 11.3
blithe 11.3
bolster 11.2
bullied 4.1
carcinogens 5.3
carcinoma 5.3
centennial 4.3
chastened 11.3
cherish 11.3
chronic 5.1, 5.3
coaxed 6.1
colonial 11.1
commiserate 4.2
commission 4.2
commitment 6.1
commotion 10.3, 11.1
compelled 4.3

compensate 6.3
competent 2.3
competence 5.1, 9.2
confirmed 10.3
constraints 2.1
constricted 6.3
consumer 6.2
contracting 11.1
convenient 4.1
conventional 9.2
cooler 10.3
core 6.2
critical 4.1
crux 9.3
dapper 10.3
davenport 4.2
de-emphasis 9.3
debris 9.1
decanter 4.2
deceptive 9.1, 10.1
demographic 6.2
depriving 4.1
dilated 6.3
dire 4.3
discriminating 2.1
dissenting 11.2
distracting 10.1
dominated 6.2
dredged 2.2
duration 6.3
encounter 5.1
entitlement 11.3
ethnicity 11.2
excessive 5.1
extracted 10.1
extradition 10.1
fashion plate 10.3
fatalities 2.2
financier 10.1
flocked 2.2
flotsam 2.2

forages 2.1
forefront 6.2
forfeit 11.1
fortitude 4.2
frailties 5.1, 5.2
fraudulent 5.2
frivolous 11.3
galvanized 4.3
garner 6.2
gauging 6.2
gawk 2.2
gaze 6.3
grappling 11.3
grievances 9.3
guile 5.2
hefty 2.1
hot grog 10.2
humdrum 9.2
hygienic 9.3
idling 4.1
imminent 2.2
impulse 11.1
incarceration 2.3
inconsistencies 11.2
incorruptible 4.2
indigenous 11.2
inducement 6.1
industrialists 11.2
insight 4.2
insomnia 10.2
inspired 9.3
intolerance 2.1
intuitive 6.3
irrational 6.1
languish 6.1
lard 2.1
liberated 9.1
limp 10.1
lymph 5.3
maligned 2.1
manipulations 10.1

migration 11.2
mingled 10.3
minutiae 11.3
monetary 5.2
morbid 4.2
mutations 5.3
naturalist 11.1
oncology 5.3
oppressive 4.3
opt 2.1
osteosarcoma 5.3
paradox 4.1
pathology 5.3
perceive 6.3
perishable 5.2
perspective 5.1
pertinent 4.2
pervasive 5.1
phony 5.2
pinnacle 9.3
plummeted 2.2
podium 4.3
positioned 6.2
pout 9.2
precipitation 9.1
premise 6.1, 9.3
previous 10.3
pristine 2.1
profound 5.1, 6.3
proponent 9.3
psychosis 2.3
recanted 4.3
recrimination 11.3
reluctantly 10.3
resonant 4.3
resort 6.1
rotary 9.1
rural 9.2
scalpers 11.2
scenario 2.3, 6.1
schizophrenic 2.2
sediment 2.2
self transcendence 5.1
severity 2.3
sleight 5.2
spacious 11.1

spectators 9.2
spurious 4.3
stashed 10.1
steeled 11.3
stereotype 9.2
stifled 9.3
strive 6.2
strolled 10.3
subtle 9.2
summon 11.1
surmised 2.3
sweltering 4.3
swindle 5.2
symbolizes 4.1
synchronized 4.1
timidity 5.1
took-a-dive 2.3
torrential 9.1
trance 10.1
tranquil 9.1
trauma 5.3
trend 6.2
trigger 2.1
unconscious 4.1
veranda 11.1
verbalizing 9.3
vigilance 6.1
wading 10.3